TALKING TO CHILDREN ABOUT MENTAL HEALTH

The challenges facing Gen Z and
Gen Alpha and how you can help

Lily-Jo

For Dave, Dylan and Nico –
love you for ever xxx

First published in Great Britain in 2023

Society for Promoting Christian Knowledge
36 Causton Street
London SW1P 4ST
www.spck.org.uk

British Library Cataloguing-in-Publication Data
A catalogue record for this book is available from the British Library

ISBN 978–0–281–08782–2
eBook ISBN 978–0–281–08783–9

1 3 5 7 9 10 8 6 4 2

Typeset by Fakenham Prepress Solutions, Fakenham, Norfolk NR21 8NL
First printed in Great Britain by Clays Ltd

eBook by Fakenham Prepress Solutions, Fakenham, Norfolk NR21 8NL

Produced on paper from sustainable sources

Contents

About the author

Lily-Jo is the founder and director of award-winning mental health platform <www.thelilyjoproject.com>. The Lily-Jo Project aims to eliminate the stigma of mental ill health by providing resources, promoting awareness and empowering people to take control of their mental well-being. She is also a singer-songwriter and qualified counsellor and counselling supervisor with more than a decade of experience.

Introduction
You need to know

You need to know you're beautiful in every single way.
Why don't you know?
You're worthy, don't let anybody take it away.
Lily-Jo, song 'Need to know'

The girl lingered behind a group of teenagers who were pressing close to me, holding their phones up at just the right angle above us for a selfie. I remember being hot from dancing under the stage lights, having just finished a full show. I was tired but happy to meet these young people, who had jumped and laughed their way through the event. The group moved on its way and I gave my familiar goodbye of, 'Thanks for coming! Follow us on Snapchat!'

Then I turned to the girl. She had long sleeves and her eyes were red-rimmed from crying. She was mumbling slightly, telling me that she had something to give to me. Then she dropped several small objects on to my waiting palm. Light to hold, sharp-edged, with a flash of silver. My stomach lurched as I realized what they were. I looked down at the razor blades then up at her.

'I want you to have them,' she said, tugging her sleeves self-consciously. 'I don't want to hurt myself any more, because of what you sang, because of what you said. No one's ever talked about it like that before . . . '

She nodded towards the razor blades as she spoke – blades that she had used to hurt herself, now given to me, like a promise that the future would be better.

'Anyway, I want you to have them.'

That moment changed my life. It was the moment the Lily-Jo Project – an online mental health resource and schools education programme – was born.

***

In the year 2015, I was living my dream. I was part of a band that was touring the world and, every night, I got to sing on stage, truly alive and thriving on the applause and the incredible feeling of thousands of people knowing the words to our songs. I also had the great joy of singing songs about self-worth and confidence, written to help those in our audience understand their true value.

As I became more confident and felt comfortable about my place in the band, I started to bring a little of my day job into our performances. I had qualified as a counsellor in 2011, so liked to share some mental health titbits from the stage, hoping to help our mostly teenage audience members to navigate the hardships of life. Little did I know then that those titbits would open a floodgate of young people sharing their stories of struggle and their mental health journeys. Their experiences brought a certain realization into sharp focus: *no one was talking about mental health.*

Just like the girl who gifted those precious, terrible razor blades to me, more and more young people came forward after shows, offering up their stories, which had as a common theme the silence that was dominating our culture. No one was telling these young people key truths: that they were loved, they were valuable and there was help out there for them.

All I had were my songs, my counsellor training and the gnawing feeling that if something didn't change in terms of how we talked about mental health, there would soon be an epidemic of self-harm. One young girl had given me her razor blades, but how many more young people still held on to theirs, risking their well-being and even their lives? How many young people could we lose? I had to do something. I wanted to turn that pain into something beautiful.

***

I know what it is like to be held back by struggles with mental health. In 2006, a trauma catapulted me into a previously unknown world of low mood, sadness and hopelessness. Before that, I had no awareness of mental ill health. Mental illness wasn't talked about in school, so I had no way to even imagine that what I was struggling with so much was post-traumatic stress disorder (PTSD). I thought that mental ill health was for 'other people'. I was hurting, but the pain I felt was also everything I knew – it was safe, my comfort blanket, and I thought that I would be losing something if I gave it up. I was wrong. I was lucky that my mum suggested counselling, which helped me to understand and process my emotions.

Counselling also unlocked my potential and set me on my career path. Learning that we all have to look after our *mental* health – just as we do our physical and emotional health – changed my perspective entirely. Now, I travel around the world sharing my experiences and knowledge as a counsellor to help reduce the stigma of mental ill health, yet I know how easily things could have been very different.

According to the NHS, one in four adults and one in ten children will experience a mental health problem in England each year,[1] and these numbers reflect a global trend. Yet, despite how common it is, nine out of ten people with mental health problems say that the stigma and discrimination associated with mental ill health have a negative impact on their lives.[2] Further, suicide is the biggest killer of young men in the UK, and the highest rate of suicide across all genders and age groups worldwide occurs among men in the 45 to 49 age group. Globally, a person commits suicide every 40 seconds.[3] On average, in the UK alone, 12 men a day take their own lives.[4] When I look at those statistics, I can't help but wonder what kind of mental health education those 12 men received at school. I can't help but consider that we, as a society, failed them.

We need to make significant changes to our understanding to stop those patterns repeating. Yes, it's true that I'm now part of a rapidly growing 'mental health industry' that is seeking to destigmatize mental health conditions worldwide and provide positive, affirming education, so there has been some progress, but the statistics show we still have a long way to go. For example, 10 per cent of our children and young people struggle with mental health problems, yet 70 per cent of them do not receive sufficient intervention at a young age.[5] Young people do have more access to services, more education and more awareness of their own mental health than has been the case ever before, but the truth is that our children and young people are also facing unprecedented challenges.

During the COVID-19 pandemic, we were plunged into not only a global health crisis but also a defining mental health crisis for our youngest generations. They have had to contend with growing up in a global landscape forever changed by the pandemic and manage to do so online in a technological revolution that is moving at the fastest pace in history while also staring down the barrel of an oncoming climate crisis. All those things are factors that could possibly be contributing to the ongoing rise in emotional disorders (such as anxiety and depression) among children and young people, which have increased by 48 per cent since 2004.[6] I have made a commitment, not only as a mental health practitioner and advocate but also as a parent, to increase my understanding of these contributing factors and share what I learn with others.

Our world is changing, my children are growing up in a way that is so different from my upbringing, and I know many other parents feel the same way. It's important that our solutions for helping them with their mental health reflect those changes. My son was born in 2007. That means he is at the tail end of Gen Z, which is the name given to anyone born between 1995 and 2009. My daughter is part of Gen Alpha. It has been so insightful for me, both as a parent and as a person who works with young people, to investigate the social, political and economic differences between my own generation and those my children belong to. Before starting to write this book, I was aware of how my children's lives were different from mine at their age, but I had not really thought about why they were. I had never considered that, in the course of my son's life so far, the word 'cloud' has completely changed its meaning. As parents, we know that our children are the online generation, but I have become more aware of what that means: our children have *never* been offline. My son was born in the same year that the first iPhone came out (2007). He has no experience of a world in which phones were not connected to the Internet and carried around in our pockets. I would be foolish, both as a mental health professional and as a parent, to try to present mental health insights that do not take into account the overwhelmingly online culture in which young people exist today. There are many connections between living life online and mental health problems, and I shall explore them in the coming chapters, but it is also very important that we do not demonize technology.

It's so easy to look at the world my children are growing up in, where technology is at their fingertips every moment of the day, and compare it unfavourably to what it was like in my own childhood. It can be easy to stereotype them as 'tech-obsessed', just as millennials have been stereotyped as lazy and baby boomers before them as entitled. No one likes to be stereotyped, yet it is easy to look at the problems facing young people today and think that somehow it is down to them.

Often, when I talk to parents about young people's mental health, they cite social media and technology as the driving force behind the undeniable numbers of them who experience poor mental health. I understand why. Even as a fairly 'cool' parent (!), I still feel anxious about my children and technology. I am still prone to blaming social media and online gaming for their bad moods and outbursts. I still catch myself on the brink of starting a sentence with the dreaded, 'In my day, . . . '. The challenge I want to offer in this book, however – for myself and other caregivers – is this: how can changing our assumptions about younger generations and how they interact with technology on a daily basis help us to understand their mental health problems more accurately?

I firmly believe that, even though the problems our children and young people are facing in the coming century are complex and nuanced, our approach to their mental health should be based on practical, simple solutions they can remember and understand. I don't expect us all to become counsellors or mental health experts overnight, but I do believe we can provide excellent support and education for our children, youth groups, students and young people today based on a true understanding of what they need. Together, we can create safe communities in which they can be educated, nurtured and learn to thrive without the shadow of stigma relating to mental health problems.

The knowledge that I share in this book can help you to support the children and young people in your care and really understand what it is they are facing. I'll show you practical ways to engage with them and, at the end of each chapter, I have provided a template for an exercise you can use to support your child's or young person's mental health, alongside journal prompts and action points for you to record your own learning. When we begin to look at the mental health of those around us, we also begin to take notice of our own mental health journeys. My hope, therefore, is that the practical applications you will find in this book will be something which benefits your own mental health as well as that of your child or young person.

This book, ultimately, has been a labour of love. The love I feel for my own children, but also the compassion I feel every time I teach a class about mental health, lead an assembly on self-esteem or sing a song about self-worth. The journey this book will take you on is one of love too. All that I have learnt about our children and young people has only increased my desire to give them the support they truly deserve, and that passion fuels my work. I know that it will fuel you also. One of my favourite quotes is by Thich Nhat Hanh, from *How to Love* (Parallax Press, 2015): 'Understanding someone's suffering is the best gift you can give another person. Understanding is love's other name.' I am excited to get started on this journey of understanding that, ultimately, leads us to support, listen to and love the children and young people in our lives in the way they deserve.

***

Please visit <www.thelilyjoproject.com/book> for bonus content, updates and to share your thoughts and experiences.

1

Generation AO
Loneliness and life lived online

I'm saying a prayer
And there's somebody there who's waiting
And waiting to say these words to you
To you: You're not alone.
Lily-Jo, song 'Never Alone'

When I was a teenager, I loved being connected to others. At 15, I had a landline phone installed in my room. I remember chatting to my friends for 59 minutes exactly before hanging up and starting again – any longer and we would be charged! It was our way to combat loneliness, our way to see one another through the tough times when talking to our parents and teachers seemed impossible. It seems strange to me, therefore, that, now, technology – the thing that, in the magical form of a landline phone, enabled me to experience so much connection and reduced my loneliness – may be the very thing that is now having the opposite effect, causing loneliness in young people.

Statistics show us that young people today are lonelier than were those of previous generations, especially in the wake of the pandemic.[1] A YouGov poll in the autumn of 2020 showed that half of 18- to 24-year-olds felt lonely during the lockdown, and 69 per cent of adolescents felt alone 'often' and 'sometimes'.[2] Those findings reflect the results of other studies carried out in the USA and elsewhere in the wake of the pandemic. To compare, the results of a pre-pandemic survey, in 2019, were that 88 per cent of 18- to 24-year-olds said they experienced loneliness to some degree, with a quarter of them saying they were suffering it often. If we compare those statistics with those for people aged 55, we can see a significant difference: only 7 per cent of 55-year-olds said that they were suffering from loneliness often, and just 2 per cent said they were lonely all the time, compared to 7 per cent for 18- to 34-year-olds.[3]

We know that loneliness can increase social isolation and make young people more vulnerable to mental health problems, such as depression and anxiety. There are many reasons why they may feel lonely – family, friends and pressures from others at school are among some of the top instigators of situations and so on that cause this to come about. It would be irresponsible, however, not to examine how being part of Generation Always On (Generation AO – that is, always having lived an online life), may relate to loneliness. A study in 2016 showed that half the teenagers interviewed felt that they were addicted to their phones,[4] and a connection has been made between digital addiction and loneliness – sometimes called 'phoneliness'.[5] Could it be that living an online life is causing digital addiction in our children and contributing to their loneliness?

As mentioned earlier, I believe that it is incredibly important for us as adults not to demonize technology, as it is something that we cannot cut from our children's and young people's lives in any real way. As we take the time now to look deeper into the connection between living life online and loneliness, we need to remind ourselves that it is not technology in itself that causes loneliness. Rather, it is how we integrate it into our lives and manage its impact that affects us. With that thought in mind, let's look at the facts.

Is phone/screen addiction real?

Working in schools as much as I do, the children and young people often share stories with me and my team. One time, a member of my team was working with a young person who told us about what he had done at the weekend. He and his brother had been sitting playing video games for two days. They had barely eaten, they had hardly slept and they had even soiled themselves rather than disconnect from their devices. They were between the ages of eight and twelve. This story turned out to be part of a wider narrative of chronic parental neglect that the school and social services were already aware of, but hearing it reminded me of something very important about phones, screens and other digital devices: children and young people are not equipped with the same abilities to control impulses that we have developed as adults. I realized that often we expect them to self-regulate their use of technology in a way that we would never do with other addictive substances. That is because we do not recognize the impacts digital addiction can have on our brains.

Research has shown us that the mental stimulus we receive from push notifications, scrolling and clicks is reinforced by an elevation in the levels of dopamine in the brain – the happy hormone. Apps and games are designed in such a way that they grab our attention, then reward that attention with things we enjoy.[6] For instance, if a child or young person is playing a game on a phone, the game will be using a simple attention-reward model, whereby if a task is completed, a reward is given in the game and that gives the child a little boost of dopamine.

That kind of reaction to apps and games isn't addictive in itself, as we also get little dopamine boosts when we win a football match, complete a chore at home or are given a promotion. Dopamine, however, is a hormone that we release in anticipation of something good happening. It helps our brain to remember the experience and catalogue it as something that we want to repeat. With gambling, for instance, we may get a rush from winning some money on a slot machine and so our brain catalogues it as a positive experience. As adults, however, we also have a whole host of knowledge about gambling and its addictive qualities that help us to control future urges to gamble. We might decide to ignore those warnings, but we have them.

With digital devices and online games, however, we do not think that knowledge applies. We don't log on to an app and expect it to be set up like a casino. We don't realize that, as we scroll through a social media site, essentially, we are pulling the lever on a slot machine and waiting for the bell to ring, but in the app, the 'bell' is an amusing post or a funny video. That is why it can be so easy to lose hours of your life to endless scrolling.

As adults, generally, we have the self-awareness to identify addictive behaviours in ourselves. For instance, I have noticed that if I am deep in scrolling on Instagram and one of my children interrupts me, my instinctive reaction can be to feel irritated. That is because my brain has been enjoying a reward-based bath of dopamine and I'm being pulled out of it. As an adult, I can look at the situation and recognize what's happening to my behaviour. A child, though, can't do that, and for teenagers, it can be even harder.

My son loves to play video games. In my family, we have noticed that, sometimes, even though he enjoys it, playing it can make him highly strung and irritable. When researching this book, I came to the realization that it is not the game alone which causes the behaviour; it also has to do with his teenage brain chemistry. It turns out that teenagers have what is called 'dopamine sensitivity'.[7] That means our young people's developing brains are more likely to react to dopamine than adults' brains and they are less likely to recognize the consequences of their behaviour as dangerous or risky. This is part of the reason why adolescents are often characterized as engaging in reckless behaviour. It is not that they don't know the risks, it's that their sensitivity to dopamine means they consider the risks less important than adults do. For that reason, teenage brains are also more sensitive to picking up patterns, especially in reward-based systems. It also means that teenagers are more vulnerable to becoming addicted and so reward-based systems – Facebook, Snapchat, TikTok, online gaming and so on – are going to be more potentially addictive for them than they are for adults, and they can be pretty addictive for adults.

Learning this, I realized that my son's irritability is not just behavioural or social, it is also chemical. When I make him stop playing to come to dinner, I am interrupting a cycle of dopamine inside his brain that he is enjoying. This drove it home to me how important it is for adults to take responsibility for teaching children how to interact healthily with reward-based apps and games, especially as it can lead to an addiction that can have long-term impacts on their mental health.

Does digital addiction cause loneliness?

Addiction in itself does not cause loneliness. After all, most of us could admit to some degree of addictive dependency on the drug caffeine, but it does not make us definitively lonelier than those not similarly addicted. In a study involving university students, it was found that those who used their phones the most were the ones who also reported the highest levels of loneliness, isolation and depression.[8] Those things are not caused by the phones themselves or alone, however. Constant connection to an online world can lead to disconnection from social groups, causing isolation. Isolation is a big factor in loneliness or 'phoneliness'.

When I first looked into 'phoneliness', I was amused by the idea but, as I investigated further, it echoed a lot of what I experience with my own phone/social media use and my children's habits. 'Phoneliness' is a type of loneliness unique to how a person feels when online.

Research shows us that, initially, using social media makes us feel less lonely. There is a tipping point, however, of between 30 minutes and an hour a day. After that, we either cease to feel the benefits of social media on our loneliness or begin to experience *increased* loneliness.[9] I found that this happened to me with social media. When I just checked my Instagram and Facebook for five minutes a day, I was rewarded with news, comments and new information, and felt connected to the world. Yet, when I allowed myself to be constantly connected, always checking, I began to feel less satisfied and more depleted. That is because, after a certain point, I am no longer using social media in a way which could really be described as social. As I scroll endlessly through other people's posts, waiting for possible messages or reading advertisements, I am no longer participating, I am only watching. It's at that point, I believe, social media stops being social. Something that is meant to connect us is no longer offering connectivity.

In our own survey of young people aged between 11 and 18, we found a quarter of participants agreed that social media made them feel lonely, but when asked if it also made them feel connected to others, over 80 per cent agreed that it did.[10] It is not just that screen addiction has an impact on some and not others, it's that it can have an impact on us all at different times and to different degrees. In that way, it is much like sugar and, in my house, it is treated much the same. It's not inherently bad for us, but too much of it may make us feel bad.

As with sugar, it would take a crusade against the very foundations of our existing culture to cut out screens, the Internet, phones and online life entirely. All the children in my daughter's primary school class have online avatars who receive rewards for good behaviour. Children and young people can hardly be expected to detach themselves from all such forms of online socialization when it even makes up part of their classroom learning. As caretakers, then, we must tackle protecting their mental health from the implications of screen addiction in the same way that we tackle protecting their physical health from the influence of sugar: with *healthy boundaries.*

Practical guide to setting boundaries – four top tips

Be kind to yourself

Let me begin by being perfectly honest: boundaries are never flawless. As parents and caregivers, we go in with the best intentions, but there is always something that makes it harder – a global pandemic, for instance. I am the first to put my hand up and say that lockdown blurred a lot of the boundaries we had set for all the best reasons. How can you enforce a rule of an hour of screen time a day when your children must spend between four and six hours a day online with their teachers? I can't pretend that I didn't let rules slip, because I did, and I don't think there is shame in that. We all adapted to an impossible situation. I will say, however, that the boundaries we had in place before lockdown began definitely helped us to keep a handle on things during it.

Every child is different, and implementing rules at any stage of a child's life can be difficult, yet the research doesn't lie: while connecting online has its benefits, unregulated use for unlimited amounts of time is a potential contributor to loneliness, isolation, depression and anxiety. For that reason, I have shared four practical solutions that can help you on your way to setting boundaries for your children and young people to enable them to flourish both online and offline.

1 Set clear device deadlines

Since time is one of the biggest factors contributing to screen addiction and consequential mental health problems, I see tremendous value in setting time limits on device use inside the home. It can be really valuable to have a two-way discussion with your child or young person about what amount of time is reasonable and at what times of the day. My children both enjoy coming home from school and using their devices to decompress for an hour or two before dinner. When they understand that they can only have use of their devices for a limited time, then it is important to allow them to do this at the time when it gives them what they need – it may be communicating with friends, playing games or watching TV to calm down and relax.

Something that we have found valuable is to accept their choices regarding how they use their device time without judgement (within reason – apps and websites should be age-appropriate, for example). It is important not to shame children and young people for enjoying technology as, unless you never watch TV to relax or enjoy a trip to the cinema, it is hypocritical! Studies show that children and young people are much more likely to respect boundaries if they feel that they are logical and reasonable, and if they see the values behind the boundaries also being respected by their parents.

2 Create phone-free zones

One of the easiest ways to limit your child's or young person's connection to social media and online gaming is to create physical spaces in your home where phone usage is not allowed. In our house, the children are not allowed phones upstairs, because there we only have bedrooms and the bathroom. The benefit of having the children's bedrooms as a phone-free zone is that we know looking at a phone right before bed can affect our sleep cycles. This only affects my son, as he is the only one old enough to have a phone. It is mainly to provide him with some distance from social media, messaging apps and online games, all of which include a reward-based formula that is especially engaging and potentially addictive to teenagers.

If it is not possible for you to create phone-free physical zones in your home or space, you can try creating phone-free social zones. For example, in our household, we don't allow phones at the dinner table. That means we create a time in the day when phones are not allowed and we communicate together as a family. That leads me to my next practical suggestion.

3 Find offline together time

Prioritize time when you are all away from your devices and give one another attention. Without devices, especially initially, you may find that it can be hard to keep a conversation going, especially if everyone is tired from a hard day and some of your group are surly teenagers! In our house, our practice is to add to 'gratitude lists' at dinner time, which is a phone-free zone. We go around the table, each of us saying something that we are grateful for.

As a parent, I also have my five 'not fine' questions. Anyone who has had a conversation with a child or young person knows that if you ask the question, 'How was school/how was your day?', you will receive only one dreaded answer: 'Fine.' It is incredibly frustrating for the parent or caregiver, but also for the child. To avoid this conversational black hole, I have five questions that I ask.

- Who did you play with/who did you hang out with today?
- What was the best part of your day today?
- Who got in trouble today and why?
- What games did you play today?
- What was your best subject today?

If dinner times do not work for you as a family, perhaps you can find another time to prioritize non-screen socializing with your child or young person. I have found that, even as our children enter their teenage years, I still prioritize bedtime as a time when we are all off our devices and we can catch up on their days. I often find that those are the times when they are most likely to tell us something about their personal feelings or mental health because they know they have our full attention. Offline together time is not about healthy boundaries only for the children; it is also about healthy boundaries for us. We need to demonstrate to our children that we are capable of honouring their conversations by giving them our full, undivided attention.

4 Balance IRL connections and URL connections

All my suggestions are about balance, and one of the most important ways to give our children and young people balance in an online world is by creating IRL (in real life) opportunities for them. My son loves to play online games with his friends, but, equally, he loves to play basketball.

One of the hardest parts of the pandemic for our family was that all our IRL connectivity with the outside world was limited instead to purely URL (online) connections. We lost all our school clubs, family gatherings and adventures with friends. It made me so aware of how valuable that time outside the house and offline was for my children's sense of balance – and my own.

It is not about limiting a child's or young person's online time, however, but, rather, limiting the amount of their available time that they can spend online. If my son comes home from school and has basketball in the evening as well as homework, he does not have extra time beyond his one or two hours of screen time to long for more. That is why it is sometimes those young people in the older echelons of Generation Z, those who are at university or have moved out of the family home, who experience the highest levels of loneliness as a consequence of screen addiction. They are lacking the formal structure of school, extracurricular activities and family environments. For those young people, creating their own structure for each day can be invaluable. We have therefore suggested a structure to help young people in that position find balance in their lives.

Summary

In this chapter, we have discussed the importance of having and establishing digital boundaries with the children and young people in your care. We also discussed the impact of modelling good boundaries for them by what we do in our own lives.

Self-reflection question

What kind of digital boundaries do you have in your life?

Self-reflection activity

Make a list of all the ways in which you engage with technology and when your screen time can be witnessed by the children or young people in your care. Do you look at your phone at the dinner table? What are your screen-time habits? Analyse them. What do those habits say about your digital boundaries?

2

Anxiety gone viral
Anxiety and cancel culture in Gen Z

I know you want to be
The person in the picture who's got it all together
But if you only could see
You don't need no filter.
Lily-Jo and Philippa Hanna, song 'Known'

My son would not wear his new coat to school. I couldn't understand it. He had saved all his pocket money, all his earnings from various odd jobs, to buy his designer coat. It was more than I'd thought reasonable to spend, but it was his money and I was happy to see that he was saving and being wise with his finances. He was so excited to buy the coat, so eager to wear it to school for the first time and now, after only one day, he was refusing to wear it again.

After much cajoling and interpretation of shrugs and winces that parents and carers are so good at, I worked it out. Someone had said something nasty about his coat, his carefully saved-for and much-desired coat. Now he wouldn't wear it. I am sure we all remember similar times in adolescence when someone said something to you that wormed its way deep into your heart or psyche and changed the way you dressed or acted.

This, however, felt different to me. For my son, the need to keep up the performance of what was 'appropriate' among his peers didn't end at the school gates, it followed him home. He couldn't wear the coat in public *ever again* because living online meant that there was no escape from the constant performance for his peers. For young people today, that constant need to perform in every area of their lives is, unsurprisingly, having an impact on their mental health.

Anxiety is one of the biggest mental health problems facing Gen Z today. While 43 per cent of people in the UK have experienced anxiety and panic attacks, young people are 17 per cent more likely to suffer from anxiety and panic attacks than those in other age groups.[1] In the first year of the pandemic, a global study showed that anxiety in young people rose by at least 20 per cent.[2]

In our research with young people, we have found that one of the largest causes of their anxiety relates to academic achievement.[3] That makes sense when we consider young people today are not only performing at school but also online on a potentially global scale. I was only a student for two years. I moved out of my parents' house when I was 18, and I was financially independent from them by the time I was 19. I didn't go to university straight out of school, but that wasn't abnormal for my class. The future looks very different for my children.

Research shows us that my children will be in the 'student' stage of life longer than any previous generation. It is predicted that one in two Gen Alpha children will have a university degree.[4] Comparatively, only 25 per cent of my parents' generation have one.[5] Gen Alpha children will live at home longer, enter the workforce later and likely have delayed financial independence. That means there is an increased amount of pressure on making those academic investments worthwhile. Unsurprisingly, it creates anxiety that comes out in panic attacks, insomnia and disordered eating – all common side effects of anxiety.

It doesn't seem like school is at the core of the problem, however. When speaking to Morgan, a 15-year-old student, they said:

> Most of my friends' biggest worries come from school. We all have a lot of stress and anxiety about . . . the future. We are all worried about the grades we will get and what people will think.

It is being worried about 'what other people will think' that is at the core of Gen Z's anxiety. It's performance anxiety and it's not only limited to the classroom. My son won't wear his coat not only because of what might be shouted out in the playground but also what might happen if someone took a picture of him and then put it online.

Anxiety around online backlash is high for adolescents. Our own data shows us that nearly 60 per cent of our interviewees worry about embarrassing themselves online.[6] The fear of getting it wrong, of not being cool enough, woke enough and smart enough is plaguing our young people, particularly at school and online.

The question I want to ask is: why? I believe that it is because of the culture being created around them: 'cancel culture'.

How does cancel culture make us anxious?

A couple of years ago, I opened Instagram to find that someone had set up a fan account. I was so surprised and humbled to see it, clicking on to the app while on the bus to a venue with my team, and I had a lovely conversation with the person running the account. They had seen me perform and loved my work. It was astonishing and gratifying, the feeling of being seen and recognized. I got off the bus and went on with my day, not realizing that I had been sent a message from the fan account that I had not replied to.

Some 20 minutes later, I checked Instagram again. The fan account was now a hate account. I hadn't responded to the message and the creator had taken that as a sign of my lack of interest. They had renamed the account to express their dislike of me, complete with skull and dagger emojis. I was shocked at first and then afraid.

It had only taken 20 minutes, but it was enough time to drive home to me the fickle nature of our online presence.

I had gone from being celebrated to being 'cancelled' by someone. My anxiety was not only that someone had used vivid and alarming images to express their sudden violent dislike of me but also what such public cancellation would do to my online presence, my career and, ultimately, my life.

The term 'cancel culture' emerged around 2017 as a way to describe public outcry over an individual's unacceptable behaviour. The instance that stands out the most for me was the public reaction to the trials of Harvey Weinstein for rape and sexual assault, which, in turn, fuelled the #MeToo movement.

For many young people today, cancel culture is a part of how they protest about injustice. When speaking with my young friend Morgan, they explained:

> We are more of a community, a lot more of us understand about mental health. If we see a person who is acting terribly, we'll call them out. Previous generations don't seem to do that. We want to stand up and support the victim, even if that means ganging up on the offender.

For young people like Morgan, their online life gives them more control over the world. They know that 'cancelling' people (writing about them negatively online, refusing to endorse them or purchase products associated with them) has an impact on their ability to do their job or live well.

They understand that power of the cancel. It can also have an adverse effect on the cancellers, however: they are anxious about being cancelled themselves.

Compared to their millennial counterparts, therefore, Gen Z are much more reserved about what they post online. They prefer image-based platforms – TikTok, Snapchat – to Twitter and Facebook, as their focus is on 'sharing' rather than 'speaking'.[7] They value digital privacy and anonymity more too. Gen Z and Gen Alpha children are less likely to post photos of themselves, for instance – a trend that I have seen in my own life. While my own Facebook and Instagram are littered with photos of friends and family, my nieces and nephews never post anything personal on TikTok. Gen Z are, and probably the generation coming afterwards will be as well, aware of the impact of 'messing up' online. For the children who do so, though, the consequences are not likely to be the loss of a huge social media following or connected to their career. They are more likely to be much closer to home and personal. I'm talking about 'cyberbullying'.

How does cyberbullying increase anxiety?

Cyberbullying is not worse than what we might call 'normal' bullying. Speaking to children and young people in schools, the impact of bullying is always detrimental to their self-esteem and mental health, whether it happens online, in school or at home. Cyberbullying is distinctive, however, because it might never stop. Cyberbullying means that the cruelty can follow children wherever they go, as long as they have a device connected to the Internet.

We have also noticed from conversations with children and young people in schools that there tends to be more of a 'pile on' mentality with online bullying. For instance, in a classroom or playground, there will always be some who are reticent about joining in with bullying tactics for fear of getting caught. The veil of anonymity available to them online, however, takes that fear away, making it easier for them to be cruel. For instance, during the pandemic, when children and young people were spending even more time online than usual, studies show that there was a 70 per cent rise in hate speech (cyberbullying) between children and young people during online chats, and a 40 per cent increase in toxicity on popular gaming platforms, such as Discord.[8] That's a stunningly high increase, and it's because it is easy to be cruel when you literally don't have to face the consequences of your actions.

Sometimes I like to go running and sometimes I invite my son. He rarely joins me because he is afraid of being 'seen looking stupid'. It's not because he is vain or too focused on appearances, but because he has grown up in a world where one 'mistake', one instance of not being seen as 'cool', can have seemingly endless consequences. Someone might snap a picture or make a comment online.

Someone might find that funny. It might snowball and, suddenly, before he knows it, people he's never met or heard of before – friends of friends of friends – are making negative comments about him without thinking how that will make him feel. In a few clicks, harmless comments become cyberbullying.

How can we find it surprising that children and young people are so anxious about what others think of them when the thoughts of others have the potential to make their lives utterly miserable? If I, as an adult, was anxious that one hate account would have an impact on my career, how much more anxious will children and young people with no power be when they think about how, in every moment of every day, they might do something that will make them a pariah? Not only in the classroom but everywhere? That's the trouble with the Internet: it brings the classroom, and the people in it, into your home.

How, then, can we make it better? How can we help our children and young people maintain a balance between staying connected and managing their own anxiety? As a parent and caregiver, I know that sometimes my instinct is simply to remove the things that I think might be causing my child distress. Who could blame parents faced with the possibility of their child being 'cancelled' or cyberbullied for simply throwing up their hands and saying, 'That's it! No more Internet!' It's tempting sometimes. At such times I remind myself that *it's about my child, not the things around them.*

My youngest daughter is in Gen Alpha. They have been described as a generation of 'upagers'. This term, coined by Mark McCrindle, is used to describe how:

> physical maturity is setting in earlier for them so *adolescence will begin earlier* and so does the social, psychological, educational and commercial sophistication, which can have negative as well as positive consequences.[9] (My italics)

That means it's not the Internet, it's the world they are living in. The world is making them grow up faster and that acceleration is having an impact on their self-esteem, which is having an impact on their ability to manage anxiety. Aside from sending my children to Mars, there is no way to avoid it, so what I must do, what I am trying to do, is help them to live in this fast-paced online world as best they can and manage anxiety if and when it arises. Next are some of my tips to help children and young people live safely in the world, with confidence rather than anxiety.

Practical guide to managing anxiety – six top tips

1 Create safe spaces

We've already seen that many, many young people have the potential to be always connected and, as a result, have feelings of anxiety, of needing always to be presenting and curating their personality in the 'right' way for the world to see.

To circumvent children's and young people's need to be continually presenting so as not to feel anxious, we need to create circumstances and spaces in which that doesn't arise. This is what I call a 'safe space'. For my son, that space is his bedroom. He has a TV in there, which he can use to watch Netflix and play games on, but it is a space where he can't receive WhatsApp messages or anything else of the kind (due to the no phone zone I spoke about earlier, in Chapter 1). His room is also a space where he feels that he can truly be himself and relax. He is in perfect control of that environment and has no need to 'present' himself. It's also a space where I can talk to him honestly.

Creating safe spaces does not have to involve whole rooms; they could, potentially, be moments in the day. Perhaps on the drive to and from school or when going for a walk. You might have to set a 'no phone' zone for those 'spaces' to help children or young people to understand its purpose and open up, but there need to be spaces where they can be themselves.

2 Don't dismiss a valid concern

We probably all remember times when we were told to get over something and how dismissive and debilitating that felt. For adults who grew up before the Internet was accessible everywhere (even on the international space station!), it is easy for us to make throwaway comments such as, 'It doesn't matter what people think' or, 'It's online, it's not real.' They may all feel true to us, but they're not true for Gen Z and Gen Alpha. They have grown up seeing the impact of cancel culture, they have seen a presidential candidate brought down by her emails. They *know* it matters – they are reminded of it constantly at school in online safety and well-being courses, and warned about how future employers may view their online behaviour. Telling them the opposite will not alleviate their anxiety, merely convey that you do not understand them. Instead, try to change the language you use, which leads us to Tip 3.

3 Change lacking language to listening language

When we use listening language, we show our children or young people that we are not only hearing them but also understanding them. When they reveal their anxiety about an online comment or what other people might think of them, we can choose to respond with listening language or lacking language.

'Lacking language' is language that is lacking in the care children and young people need. Let's use the example of my son not wanting to run with me because people might see him and say something. Examples of lacking language in response to that might be:

- 'What people say doesn't matter.'
- 'Nobody is going to say that.'

- 'You're being silly.'
- 'It doesn't matter what people think.'
- 'You shouldn't listen to them.'

All such responses have the potential to come across as untrue, dismissive, blaming or lacking in perspective.

Examples of 'listening language' might be:

- 'Can you explain why you think that?'
- 'What do you worry people might say to you?'
- 'How does that make you feel?'
- 'Is there something that might make you feel safer doing it?'
- 'Nothing anyone could say would change my opinion of you.'

All those responses have the potential instead to engage my son in a conversation about how he feels. When he feels heard and understood, it is more likely that his anxiety will reduce. There is even a chance that if we speak about it and his anxiety reduces, we may be able to find a way for him to engage in the activity that makes him feel safe.

4 Provide reassurance and perspective

While it does not help children and young people in the grip of anxiety to tell them that they have nothing to be worried about, you do have a valuable perspective to offer as an adult.

Children and young people know that the Internet matters, cancel culture is real and they need to 'perform', but they also need to be reminded that other things matter too. As an adult, you can provide a valuable perspective that can reassure them of this. For instance, I often explain to the children and young people I encounter in schools that, while my social media following matters a great deal to my career, it means nothing if the person members of the public encounter in the real world isn't polite and kind and generous. I remind them that whatever people say about you online or however you present yourself, it makes no difference if your attitude and behaviour are rubbish. Reassuring children and young people that their actions matter regardless of what people might think about them will help them to develop an internal dialogue to reinforce such thinking.

5 Reinforce positive self-talk

"What will my teacher think of my grades? What will everyone think about my hair? What will people say in the group chat? What will people think of my TikTok post? How many comments will it get? How many likes?"

Young people today have grown up in a world that reinforces a type of self-talk focused on others' opinions. What we can attempt to do as adults is to encourage a type of self-talk that, instead, is focused on their own opinions.

When a child or young person says, 'I'm worried about what other people will think of me', we could ask, 'What do you think of yourself?' Here's an example of how that kind of discussion might go between me and my son:

SON: 'I'm worried about what other people will think of me.'
ME: 'What do you think of yourself?'
SON: 'I think that I'm uncool.'
ME: 'Has somebody given you evidence for thinking that?'
SON: 'Someone at school.'
ME: 'Is what they said a fact or is it an opinion?'
SON: 'An opinion.'
ME: 'What is your opinion about yourself?'

Helping children and young people to identify their own opinions from the opinions of others in such a way is a valuable step in adjusting their own self-talk. The goal is that, eventually, this process becomes internal, so that they can build resilience to thoughts that might trigger performance anxiety.

6 Practise interrupting negativity

Interrupting negative thought patterns is a distraction technique used to stop children and young people from spiralling into an anxiety attack. While all our other tips have been focused on building the kind of resilience in them that might avoid such attacks, we know they can't always be prevented from happening. It's important to be equipped to handle such events when they occur.

At the Lily-Jo Project, we teach several different distraction techniques to help children and young people through different manifestations of anxiety. We have included three here for different circumstances: exam room or classroom, bedtime, and downtime. All of them rely on the fact that anxiety spirals are like bear traps for the mind: once they start, they are difficult to get out of. It is much better, if possible, for children and young people to learn techniques that help them to head their anxiety off at the pass, reducing the number of times that their anxiety overwhelms them and inhibits their normal activities.

Exam room or classroom

In a controlled setting, where children's and young people's movements and ability to change their activity are limited, we suggest the 'five things method'. We teach them that when they feel symptoms of anxiety, they should look around the room and name five things they can see, four things they can touch, three things they can hear, two things they can smell, and one thing they can taste.

This process is called 'grounding' and, essentially, it reminds children and young people that they are in control of their body and it serves to distract them from their immediate symptoms, hopefully lessening them to a point where they can either regain control of their anxiety or seek help from a teacher.

Bedtime

For many children and young people, anxiety can prevent them from falling asleep or induce bouts of insomnia. To help with that, we suggest meditative breathing. At the Lily-Jo Project, we teach breath control from the early years all the way up to adulthood, since its benefits are universally relevant across all age groups.

Anxiety or panic causes irregular breathing, which, in turn, sends signals to the brain to be alert for danger. A body on high alert is flooded with adrenaline and will struggle to go to sleep. Practising breath control rebalances the system and sends a message to the brain that there is no danger.

While there are many breathing practices, we suggest 'four, five, six breathing' because it is easy to remember and easy to teach at all levels. To do it, you breathe in through the nose for a count of four, hold your breath for a count of five, then breathe out for a count of six. Repeating the breathing pattern at bedtime can calm the mind and allow the body to relax, ready for sleep. I also recommend it as a tool for coming out of anxiety attacks.

Downtime

If children or young people experience persistent anxiety and find that their anxious thoughts spiral during their downtime (at lunch or playtime or after school, for example), we recommend a 'distraction list'. It involves making a list of things that they enjoy doing and which fully consume their attention. The list might include gaming, colouring, playing sport, watching their favourite film or TV programme or talking with their friends. Then, if the children or young people experience anxiety during their downtime, suggest that they pick an activity from their distraction list to enjoy.

When we focus our attention elsewhere, it helps to lessen anxiety. The process also gives anxious children and young people a deeper understanding of how they can manage their anxiety on their own. When they learn that independent resilience, they are less likely to feel overwhelmed and terrorized by their anxiety.

Summary

In this chapter, we looked at the causes and impact of anxiety on the lives of children and young people today. One of the techniques that can help them to cope is to change their 'self-talk'. When it comes to challenging others' negative 'self-talk', we need to practise being able to recognize it. That starts with us.

Self-reflection question

How would you characterize your own internal 'self-talk'? Is it positive? Is it negative? Do you criticize yourself a lot?

Self-reflection activity

Take a moment to write down some of your recurring internal negative thoughts. An example might be, 'I'm not good enough.' Consider what the root of that negative thought may be. Try using the following self-enquiry questions, writing your answers and thoughts down in the same way as the example of a conversation given earlier in this chapter.

- What does your list show you that you think of yourself?
- Has someone given you evidence to think that?
- Is that a fact or an opinion?
- What is your honest opinion of yourself?

3

Pandemic pressure
Post-pandemic stress disorder

I can hear you,
I can see you,
Come out of your hiding now,
It's the right timing.
Lily-Jo, song 'Diamond'

Most of us living in the world today will be able to recall with absolute certainty where we were when the first big lockdown happened. We will all remember how it felt, suddenly to be stuck inside our homes, explaining to our children that they wouldn't be going back to school, watching all the shops close and the supermarkets run out of toilet paper. Something that I will never forget is the sudden sensation of overwhelming helplessness.

As someone who is self-employed, works with school-children and educational establishments, as well as in the music industry, it felt like the life that I had so carefully and rigorously constructed was falling apart. Gigs cancelled, schools closing, and all I could do was watch my calendar empty in front of my eyes. I remember going into the bath-room to cry to myself three times a day, not wanting my children to see my fear. Our household income relies solely on businesses founded and run by me and my husband. For us, there was no furlough and, like so many others, we found ourselves in the position of worrying about how we would put food on the table if it carried on indefinitely. The lack of power, the burden of responsibility, was nearly overwhelming. I found myself riddled with panic and the recurring thought, 'I don't want to be a parent any more. I want someone to look after *me*.'

The scariest thing about the pandemic, I found, was how it snatched away my control over my circumstances; I felt lost. Research tells us that Gen Z and Gen Alpha felt the same and it has had a detrimental impact on their mental health. Indeed, a staggering 48 per cent of Gen Z feel that COVID-19 has had an extreme or substantial impact on their life.[1] Their top emotional response to the pandemic was anxiety, at 49 per cent. A Young Minds report on mental health during the pandemic in UK schools (featuring Gen Z and Gen Alpha respondents) revealed that 83 per cent of them agreed that the pandemic was making their mental health worse. Key factors cited by young people included health concerns about friends and family, changes to structures at school or university and the loss of social interaction.[2] At the Lily-Jo Project, we found that the responses were similar when we interviewed young people.[3] A year 10 student said:

A lot of people I know had a drastic mental health downturn in the pandemic because of the lack of human interaction. Our space where we can make jokes and interact together and share our mental health concerns was gone. That was really hard and made us feel alone.

I tried to FaceTime my friends a lot during the pandemic and when we first got sent home, we were excited not to be at school, we were still chatting and joking and sharing our mental health problems, but within a week, that had all changed. Everyone started to get quiet and withdrawn. All of the communication felt awkward whereas before, it was easy.

Just as research carried out around the world supports the idea that COVID-19 has had a crushing impact on the mental health of young people, it has shown that the changes to how they were experiencing education during the pandemic also had an effect. In a survey conducted by the Office for National Statistics (ONS), 41 per cent of parents reported that they felt the well-being of the child or young person in their care was negatively affected by trying to continue their education at home.[4]

Our interviews with young people[5] went a little deeper into this issue, and a year 11 student explained how the changes in education had contributed to stress, confusion and anxiety:

We were basically told throughout the year that if we didn't do well doing online work and online school, we wouldn't get good grades and we would fail. It was fearmongering. There was so much pressure to perform. We were told our mock exams were it, that our grades would be totally based on them. It was so anxiety-inducing.

There was an air of mystery, nobody knew what could happen. It was a lot of hypothetical situations that made us feel really stressed and confused. The lack of clear communication didn't help at all.

When I heard this young person's explanation, I instantly recognized in it some of my own feelings of being overwhelmed by a lack of control. It makes sense to me that if I, an adult with control over my own life, should feel burdened and mentally stressed by the pandemic, then children and young people with significantly less control should feel those effects even more. While those effects may be described as an increase in the rates of anxiety and depression, scientists are also beginning to suggest that they may be evidence of something more: post-pandemic stress disorder.

What is post-pandemic stress disorder?

Post-pandemic stress disorder, also called post-COVID disorder, is not yet an officially recognized mental health condition. What is known so far is that the pandemic has been shown to be 'traumatic' by psychological studies, and four different groups of people have been identified as experiencing high levels of post-traumatic stress disorder (PTSD) in the aftermath of the pandemic:

- those who had COVID-19 or a near-death experience with COVID-19;
- family members or key workers who witnessed the near-death experience or death of someone with COVID-19;
- those who learnt of the near-death experience or death of a family member or friend due to the virus;
- those who witnessed the devastation of the pandemic first hand on the front lines (hospital staff, key workers, medical examiners, journalists and so on).[6]

People in those groups are exhibiting the symptoms of PTSD, as described in the *Diagnostic and Statistical Manual of Mental Disorders* (fifth edition, American Psychiatric Association, 2013), known as DSM-5, which is the standard classification of mental disorders used by mental health professionals to make diagnoses. However, researchers are also looking into how the pandemic has affected the mental health of the general population. They are looking at the impact of what they call 'vicarious traumatization', which is what we might think of as second-hand trauma. That is a particularly relevant concept in relation to the experiences of young people. A study carried out a month after the outbreak of COVID-19 in China revealed that, among home-quarantined young people, 12.8 per cent of them had the symptoms we associate with PTSD – such as anxiety, stress, suicidal thoughts and depression – and had negative coping styles for dealing with the overwhelming new emotions they were experiencing.[7]

'Negative coping styles' can mean many things, but the study suggested that the following were most prevalent among the Chinese young people who were surveyed.

- **Denial** Young people exhibiting denial may refuse to acknowledge their turbulent feelings. They may seem 'numb' and often shut down discussions about emotion with phrases such as 'I'm fine' or 'nothing's wrong'. They may also struggle to be physically affectionate. It is also possible that they may turn into a whirling dervish of energy and become obsessed with 'keeping busy'.
- **Blaming** Young people who are showing blame may either blame someone else or themselves for the event. If young people are struggling with self-blame, they may begin to show symptoms of 'hypervigilance' – that is, being overly cautious or controlling of their surroundings in an attempt to offset the guilt, fear and responsibility they feel. They may also express a lack of trust in the adults around them, which is symptomatic of a belief that they need to fix everything.
- **Social withdrawal** Young people who are socially with-drawing will often suddenly become disinterested in social events and settings that used to bring them joy, such as clubs and spending time with friends. They may also carefully avoid any situations that remind them of the trauma and seem to trust their friends and those who care for them less than they did before.
- **Disengagement** When young people are disengaged, they may struggle to cope with any situations that, for whatever reason, remind them of the trauma.

Consequently, they may have sudden, strange reactions to problematic situations or emergencies. That is because they are overwhelmed by trying to process the trauma and cannot cope with anything more on top. It may be something as simple as a change of schedule (for instance, a different person is picking them up from school) or something more directly associative (if a grandparent was lost to COVID, for example, they may have sudden reactions to anything that reminds them of the grandparent).

- **Physical symptoms of anxiety** The young people may experience flashbacks to the emotions related to the trauma and feel as though it were happening all over again in that moment. They may experience distressing nightmares or pain, nausea, sweating or trembling.

It may seem far-fetched to suggest that a child or young person you care for is struggling with PTSD symptoms. After all, PTSD is very serious – we associate it with returning war veterans or the victims of terrible abuse. It's perfectly natural to baulk at the idea that your child or young person, someone you have brought up, could be struggling with PTSD. It's really important to remember, though, that while the term PTSD is used to describe the mental health struggles of those who return from war or live through terrible assaults, that is not all it covers. It is a hugely broad diagnosis because the range of circumstances that humans can find traumatic is very broad. In fact, any situation that a human being can find traumatic can cause PTSD. It might be a car crash, an assault, giving birth or, in the case of my own personal history, a divorce in the family. It's also really important to remember that what you consider traumatic may not be what your child or young person considers traumatic. After all, how we experience the world aged four or ten is vastly different from how we experience it when we are adults.

Let me help you to imagine how something seemingly mundane or simple can be overwhelming by telling the story of a young child.

Put yourself in the child's shoes

I am seven years old. I am in year three and today I was told that I couldn't go back to school because there is a horrible illness that is making everyone sick, especially old people. I am afraid because my friend's grandma has been taken to hospital and my friend isn't allowed to go and see her. I love my own grandma so much, she is my favourite person to bake with and go to the park with and, usually, I go to her house on Thursdays. Today, my parents have told me I can't go to Grandma's house for a while because we all have to stay at home. I am excited not to go to school but I'm also nervous. My grandma is old, just like my friend's grandma, and I hear Mum and Dad talking in the kitchen about how Grandma shouldn't go out to the shops or even to walk her dog in case she gets poorly. I think about my friend's grandma in the hospital with no visitors. I don't want my grandma to go to the hospital. Who will look after her dog if she does? Who will look after my grandpa? What happens if she dies? Who will pick me up from school on Thursday? I am thinking all of these things and it is making me feel so sick inside. I feel like I might be sick all the time and when it comes to teatime, I don't want to eat my food. I like chicken nuggets a lot, but I feel so sick and I don't want to be sick. I can't make Grandma safe or take her dog to the park or help my friend's grandma in the hospital. I can't make school come back or Mum and Dad stop looking so worried, but I can do this. I can stop myself from feeling sick by not eating my chicken nuggets. I can do this one thing to make myself feel better.

From the perspective of the child's parent, all you may see is your child refusing to eat dinner and reporting feeling sick. As a caregiver, all you want is for the children or young people in your care to be well and healthy. Our instinct as adults, then, might be to try to force the child to eat again, maybe even become frustrated and angry when the child refuses to comply. It is so challenging for us – especially as adults who are also struggling with our own symptoms of stress – to recognize how disobedience, grumpiness, unwillingness and tantrums could be signs that a child or young person is struggling with symptoms of trauma. Once we do, however, once we put ourselves in the shoes of those who have even less power and control than we do, we can begin to see the signs and help to turn those negative coping styles into positive ones.

In our practical guide, next, I will demonstrate how we can encourage positive coping styles in children or young people experiencing some of the most typical symptoms of trauma.

Practical guide to managing symptoms of PTSD – five top tips

1 Managing hypervigilance

My daughter started showing symptoms of hypervigilance midway through the pandemic. For her, it was that she needed complete control of the way the furniture and décor were arranged in the living room. The most important part was recognizing the symptoms and then finding a way to live with them.

For children or young people displaying hypervigilance, one of the most unhelpful things an adult can do is to swing between hot and cold reactions – namely, being very accommodating or very dismissive. That contributes to their stress as they never know whether their controlling behaviours will be met with disinterested acceptance or angry denial. It is important that they know they can talk to you about their feelings, but also know their feelings do not completely control the circumstances. For instance, it would be remiss of me to let my daughter have the final say on everything to do with the living room as I would only be enabling her hypervigilance. Equally, dismissing and denying her the opportunity to control the space would likely only lead to her taking control of another space and hiding it from me.

What is needed is a middle ground, a way for my daughter to understand that small infringements into her area of control do not need to be a bad thing or threatening. I tried to introduce 'collaboration'. I would make changes to the room, perhaps introducing a new plant, but I would ask her opinion about where it was best to put it. Doing that still allows her a modicum of control of the room, but without reinforcing the idea it is hers alone to control.

I also try to be 'sensitive' to her reactions and give her space to process them. For instance, if I have set up laundry in the room and I know she will have a reaction to that when she comes home from school, I discuss it with her on the way home. That gives her a chance to adjust to the idea rather than being abruptly confronted with it.

2 Managing negative narratives

A child or young person who is reinforcing a negative narrative might have internalized a version of events that focuses on the negative aspects of it. For instance, if a young person is depressed about having missed exams, prom and the leaving parties at the end of secondary school, the internal narrative experienced might be saying something like, 'Life is meaningless, I'll never amount to anything now, there's no point in trying.'

There are different ways to interrupt those negative narratives. Here are a few that I have found to be successful.

- **Provide alternative milestones** If a child or young person is stuck in a negative narrative because significant childhood milestones (sitting exams, completing sixth form, going to university) have been missed, try to create an alternative milestone or ceremony that can allow for some of the necessary closure to be experienced, which helps with finding meaning in life. That might be a small ceremony with friends, a special trip or a family event.
- **Rewrite the narrative** Writing things down is a common clinical tool that helps when dealing with symptoms of trauma. I have found many of my clients feel significantly lighter after writing their own accounts of an event that has caused them pain. A strategy that can also help is to ask a child or young person to rewrite the narrative, focusing on the positive things they have learnt or understood about the world or themselves as a result of the experience. In the case of the pandemic, a child or young person could turn a narrative focused on loss into a narrative focused on community spirit and personal resilience.
- **Develop positive life statements** Ask the child or young person to write down the negative beliefs that they have about themselves following the experience of the pandemic. Then ask them to choose a positive statement that acknowledges their pain. For instance, 'life is meaningless' could become 'life is hard, but it is worth it'. Make it something they can remember or even write

on a card to put up in their room, to help to change the negative narrative into a positive one.

3 Managing excessive worry

Worry can be debilitating for a child or young person. What can be helpful is to consider some 'interrupting negativity' techniques. One that I use with my clients is called 'worry time'. I encourage clients to set aside ten minutes of the day when they are allowed to worry all they want and write down every single worrying thought that they have. Once completed, I ask them to cross out the worries that they can't control and also write down as many solutions as possible to the ones they can control. Then, once the time is up, they put aside their worry journal and are no longer allowed to worry about those things.

Another option for children can be to create a 'worry box' together. It is a box that you keep in a shared space and the children can, at any point, post into the box a worry that they have written down on a piece of paper. You then set aside a certain time in the day or week (depending on how often the children need it) to open the box and discuss the worries inside. That allows the children a set time to express their worries.

Both techniques utilize a common PTSD management technique of 'boxing' a negative or damaging experience away inside the mind so that it has less of an impact on everyday life. They are particularly suitable if a child or young person is being continually overwhelmed. It is important to remember, however, that the feelings cannot be boxed away indefinitely – it is essential to make time and space for the worries to be addressed and discussed so that the child or young person can recover.

4 Managing withdrawing

My son's reaction to lockdown was different from my daughter's. Rather than experiencing hypervigilance, my son seemed more prone to withdrawing. He struggled with feeling low and wanted to retreat from social spaces into his bedroom a lot.

When that happens, essentially, the child or young person is expressing their need for safety. It is important, therefore, not to force them to do otherwise. If we do so, we are essentially denying the child or young person access to a space in which they feel safe, meaning that they remain in spaces where they feel less safe. Not only can this contribute to a child's anxiety but it can also give them damaging messages for adulthood about advocating for spaces and environments that suit their needs. As a parent, I know how difficult that can be to acknowledge and accept. Intellectually, I know that my son feels safe in our home. As a practising counsellor, however, I also know that my son's response is not intellectual. He is not saying that he feels unsafe in our home. He is not making a comment on my skills as a parent. He is expressing that something enormous has happened in his life and it has shaken his emotional foundations. As a result, he is retreating to the space in which he feels *most safe*. My job is then to help to stabilize those emotional foundations. Here are two examples of ways in which I could do that.

- **Verbal grounding** A child or young person who feels emotionally unsafe needs reassurance regarding the things that they would usually take for granted. My son *knows* that he is safe in our home, but he needs to be told and have it reinforced in order to *feel* safe. Saying things such as, 'Mum and Dad will always do everything we can to keep you safe' may seem obvious, but they acknowledge and respond to the emotional insecurity the child or young person is currently experiencing. Other phrases might include, 'I am not afraid, I feel safe' or 'Our house is a safe place', which may also help.
- **Physical grounding** When a child or young person feels emotionally unsafe, they are often experiencing the emotional needs of their much younger selves more vividly than usual. So your ten-year-old who normally does not need much physical affection may suddenly be much more open to hugs and cuddles and holding hands at such times. That is because they are unsure how to process this strange new threat emotionally, so they may revert to their earlier childhood needs and responses. A three- or four-year-old needs physical affection to feel safe and protected from the world, so it is likely that an older child or young person who feels emotionally unsafe could experience that need again too.

5 Managing avoidance

A child or young person expressing avoidance may develop aversions to things that they normally were happy to do before the pandemic. For instance, a child may become averse to hugging family members and friends.

Much as is the case with hypervigilance, forcing the issue can not only be counterproductive but can also be traumatic. It is much better to find ways to address the issue delicately, and with children and young people, using fun can be the best way. For instance, if a child or young person refuses to hug relatives any more and you are concerned that they will develop a problem with touch, you could start to develop a fun way for them to engage without being forced to cross boundaries that make them uncomfortable. You could challenge them to come up with a new greeting routine (say a handshake but with elbows or toe touches) that they can teach their friends and family. You may like to try challenging them to confront their fear in fun ways. For instance, you could say, 'I bet you can't give Grandpa the biggest high five in the world' or 'Wouldn't it be crazy if you gave Liam a pat on the back?' Framing such challenges as games that they can choose to participate in or not is a helpful way for a child or young person to feel like they have control.

Consent is incredibly important in all such situations. If a child or young person does not willingly comply but feels forced into it, then they will not consider it their own personal victory, which is the whole point of doing it. Without that feeling of triumph, the child or young person will not start to chip away at their fear or be prompted to allow themselves the realization that perhaps they can overcome things that make them nervous.

Summary

In this chapter, we discussed the impact of the pandemic on mental health and how post-pandemic stress disorder can be a struggle for children and young people today. It is important that while trying to help young people cope with the impacts of the pandemic, we also take care of ourselves.

Self-reflection question

How would you characterize the impact that the pandemic has had on your mental health? Do you find yourself experiencing symptoms of hypervigilance, negative narratives, excessive worry, withdrawal or avoidance?

Self-reflection activity

Think back to how your mental health was before the pandemic began. Rate it out of ten. Now consider your mental health today, post pandemic. Rate it out of ten. Try to write down what it is about the pandemic that has had the most significant impact on you. Take another look through the 'Practical guide to managing symptoms of PTSD – five top tips' section of this chapter and, this time, read it with your own mental health in mind. Are there any tips that you may find helpful to put into practice to support your own mental health?

4

Bodies made digital
Self-esteem and self-harm

I see who you are
Beneath the hurt
Beneath the scars
So if you ever feel alone
Remember that you are known.
Lily-Jo and Philippa Hanna, song 'Known'

When I was a teenager in the late 1990s, it was the era of celebrity supermodels. The year I turned 15, the most famous supermodel in the world was Tyra Banks, with her sass and her curves and her *Sports Illustrated* cover with her bikini bottom pulled down so low. She was slim, she was curvy, she was sultry, she was fashionable, and she set a trend among young women all over the world. Closer to home for me were the Spice Girls, with their short skirts, crop tops and overt sex appeal. Curvy girls who showed their assets were the epitome of beauty and desirability. Unfortunately for me, at 15 I did not conform to those criteria. I'd had a growth spurt and was tall and thin and, unlike in the early 2000s (which would bring in the dawn of 'heroin chic' and ultra-thin bodies like Kate Moss's would become the height of fashion), in 1997, I didn't fit in. I was teased for it, called 'Anna' or 'rexy' (very inventive taunts about anorexia), and it didn't matter what clothes I chose to wear, I couldn't change my bone structure.

It was unpleasant but, luckily, those taunts did not damage me. I was able to survive them not because I was stronger or wiser than my peers, but because I had a supportive mental health system around me. My mum always tried to take care of my self-esteem. On days when I came home from school deflated, wishing I had the type of body that would 'fit in' with the others, my mum was there to tell me I was special and unique. No matter what happened in the outside world, at home I could bathe in my mum's assurances and rebuild my self-esteem.

It isn't like that now. Today, children and young people can't get away from the outside world so easily. The outside world follows them into their home on their phone. I could maintain a good sense of my own self-worth because I had a positive environment that I could retreat to, a space where the truth of my value was much louder than the influences of the world. For many children and young people today that is impossible.

In 2017, a 14-year-old girl took her own life.[1] An investigation into her social media accounts revealed that she had been struggling with feelings of low self-esteem and had taken to researching hashtags such as #selfharm and #suicide. Consequently, her father spoke out about the responsibilities of large tech companies to make their online spaces safer and to protect the mental health of vulnerable young people.

Not all young people's online behaviour puts intense pressure on their self-esteem, but there is an unavoidable link between social media and self-esteem, and between self-esteem and self-harm. In our own research,[2] we found that one in ten young people interviewed admitted to deliberately hurting themselves frequently, and 37 per cent of our respondents answered 'Yes' when asked if they had ever had the urge to hurt themselves.

While the secretive nature of self-abuse makes it difficult to gain data from widespread studies, the Millennium Cohort Study by University College London suggests that nearly a quarter of 14-year-olds in the UK have self-harmed.[3] That statistic reliably predicts a global trend for there to be a rise in self-harming, and a study carried out in the USA showed that at least 15 per cent of young people in the sample group had committed an act of self-harm in the past year.[4]

While it would be inappropriate and unhelpful to make blanket statements about the reasons behind young people self-harming, we can look at the data we have and see some correlations. There is evidence, for instance, that self-harming behaviour is linked to young people's self-esteem, and also, in reverse, their self-esteem is actually *lowered* by acts of self-harm.[5] According to a Young Minds study, 38 per cent of young people reported that social media has a negative impact on how they feel about themselves, and 46 per cent of female participants said that social media has a negative impact on their self-esteem.[6]

Young people with low self-esteem are more susceptible to body dysmorphia disorder (BDD), a mental health condition that causes them to become overly focused on what they perceive to be their physical flaws. In the UK, more than one in 20 girls aged from 17 to 19 have been affected by it[7] and in the USA, it is 1 in 50 people.[8]

It often goes unrecognized in young people simply because having a negative attitude to their bodies is assumed to be the norm. Teenagers are commonly moody or dissatisfied, so signs of a deeper problem are often missed, but it is important that we notice as teenagers, and some children, with BDD are at higher risk of engaging in self-harm behaviour and suicide.

There is a strong connection between low self-esteem and disorders such as BDD, and between low self-esteem and social media. Let us now take a deeper look at what it means to have urges to self-harm and how social media could be having an impact on our young people's attitudes towards it.

Where does the need to hurt come from?

For many adults who care for young people, the prospect of them deliberately hurting themselves is unbearable and hard to stomach, particularly if they are your own. It is that reaction which often contributes to the stigma surrounding self-harm. Many young people therefore shy away from speaking the truth about what they're doing, fearing rejection or that it will make the people who care about them angry. They worry that they will be viewed negatively by their peers or family. That is because the truth about why people self-harm is not widely known.

Our professional mentors at the Lily-Jo Project meet with young people who have regularly had such feelings and encountered those kinds of reactions, reporting that there is a stigma associated with self-harm. When asked about the stigma that they had experienced, one of the young people said that it was the older generations in particular who stigmatized self-harm.

> What I wish people in older generations understood is that we are not doing it for attention. It's because we feel overwhelmed. We are full of pain. We don't feel and we want to feel by physically hurting ourselves, or it's the temporary relief to reduce the pain. Self-harm is like a drug. It will only relieve your pain for a bit, it won't get to the deeper issue. It's that relief that people crave. Or they feel like they need to feel something because they have really bad depression. They just want to relieve the pain.

That young person's words are incredibly insightful, and they align with the science behind why physical pain can alleviate emotional pain. It works in that way because, while emotions are psychological, they are also physical. We all know how it feels to be angry: it is not just the rage in our mind but also in our shaking limbs, our dry throat, our racing heartbeat. That is because our brains use the same area for sensing both physical and emotional pain.

Pain is processed in a part of our cerebral cortex (behind each ear) and the anterior cingulate cortex (part of the front of the brain). They are the two areas that common pain relievers such as paracetamol target. Interestingly, a study in 2010 showed that because emotional and physical pain are processed in the same place, common painkillers can reduce some emotional pain too.[9] It's a strange phenomenon.

Given how linked emotional and physical pain are, it would make sense to assume that when someone is in emotional pain, self-harm would only increase it, that the combination of both physical and emotional pain would be too overwhelming to bear. Oddly, the fact that our perceptions of emotional and physical pain follow many of the same pathways in the brain offers self-harmers unexpected relief. Self-inflicted pain peaks, but then it lessens, and as the physical pain does, so does the emotional pain. It is exactly as the young person above explained: physical pain allows the self-harmer access to a short, 'temporary relief' from emotional pain.

The young person was also right to characterize self-harm as a 'drug'. While not classified as an 'addiction', it does follow similar patterns to other behavioural addictions, such as to sunbeds, gambling or shopping, as self-harm disrupts an individual's dopamine levels. It is also similar to an addictive drug in that people can develop a tolerance of it. The results of studies of people who self-harm reveal that those who self-harmed frequently had a higher tolerance of pain than those who didn't. In that sense, they would need to inflict more intense pain to experience the same 'relief' that they had previously enjoyed.[10] Essentially, once people make a habit of self-harming, they are likely to connect the feeling of relief from emotional pain with the self-inflicted physical pain and so feel the most relief when that physical pain is intensified.

Those who self-harm are also likely to become more self-critical. For many young people, self-harm may feel like the only option for the successful regulation of their emotions, but it often increases the likelihood of them feeling those intense negative emotions as it has an impact on their self-esteem.

How is social media connected to all this? How do we help young people living in a world where they can quickly search for #selfharm? How can we protect their self-esteem and their bodies?

Self-harm and social media

I have talked about the connection between physical and emotional pain. As a therapist and a mental health advocate,

I strongly believe that the connection between the body and emotions doesn't stop with pain. We are whole beings and our ability to cope with our emotions has a huge impact on our bodies, and what we do with our bodies has an impact on how we regulate our emotions.

It is no coincidence that self-harm is a physical symptom of emotional distress, and it is manifesting at higher rates than ever before in a generation for whom social media is more prevalent than ever before. Social media focuses on physical presence and is almost entirely driven by images. For most young people, their primary social media platforms are TikTok, Instagram and Snapchat – all of which rely on users presenting themselves physically. When making a connection between low self-esteem and self-harm, therefore, we have to talk about the impact of social media.

The Young Minds report into cyberbullying showed that 38 per cent of young people felt social media had a negative impact on their self-image. That figure was higher – at 46 per cent – for girls.[11] Social media provides spaces where young people have unlimited access to advertising and celebrity content, much of which presents an unrealistic or untrue picture of the world.

It is not just that young people look up to those creating content and aspire to be like them, it is also that they often feel the pressure to be 'perfect' in their own content creation. Some of the biggest social media influencers in the world currently are teenagers. Charli D'Amelio and others like her started off making content in their bedrooms, showcasing their talents with music, modelling and make-up. As a result of that phenomenon, young people today think of social media as not only a way to share with their friends but also a way, potentially, to make money or start a career. The statistics show that many of them think of it as a viable option for the future: 86 per cent of Gen Z and millennials surveyed would post social media content for money if they could.[12] It is hardly surprising, then, that for a generation for whom value is so often determined by how you appear on screen, young people would lean towards processing their emotions in a physical way.

There is also the impact that self-harm content has on those who are feeling emotionally vulnerable. In the past, because of the stigma surrounding self-harm, young people often kept it a secret from others. While that is never good, as it cuts them off from help, it does mean they are less likely to encounter peers who are also self-harming. In much the same way as how, after a teenage suicide, the peers of the victim are more likely to be at risk for suicide due to suicide diffusion, self-harm among teenage communities can easily spark imitations. That is because young people are still learning social constructs and are more vulnerable to being influenced. On the positive side, young people can receive immense support via the social conduits that make up their social group but, on the negative side, it can also make them more susceptible to peer influences leading them towards antisocial behaviour or suicide. For example, in 2017, the TV show *13 Reasons Why*, which included a teen suicide, aired for the first time. In the aftermath, Internet searches for 'suicide' rose by 20 per cent.[13] While there were lots of good conversations about suicide and many young people came forward to speak online about their feelings, there were also several suicides reported that mirrored the one in the show.

There is a terribly fine line between raising awareness for suicide and glamorizing it. Social media can have a similar effect. It can be used for tremendous good, allowing young people to seek support and find others like them to help them overcome mental health challenges, but it can also be used to promote self-destructive behaviour. Young people are able to engage with content that promotes suicide, self-injury and the sharing of self-harm practices. When young people feel negatively about their body and they do a search on the hashtag #selfharm, it is a real gamble as to whether they will find support or more harm.

I don't say any of this to make us feel hopeless, and I am not suggesting that we must hide young people away from bad influences and never let them use the Internet. As I mentioned earlier, Gen Z and Gen Alpha are growing up in a world where technology is completely integrated into everyday life. It is unreasonable to try to stall that integration. What we can do, however, is help our young people to build up their mental resilience and self-esteem so that they can cope with outside body pressures and regulate their emotions in healthy ways. In the following guide,

I provide some advice about how we can do that, as well as a few essential tools for helping young people who are already engaged in self-harm behaviour.

Practical guide to body positivity and emotional regulation – five top tips

1 Change your compliments

Since a high proportion of young people who self-harm struggle with body dissatisfaction, it is important that we try to change the culture encouraging that dissatisfaction. We can do that, in part, by altering our language.

Children and young people today are growing up in a world where physical commentary is everywhere. We need to demonstrate that we do not assign worth based on what they look like or wear, but on who they are, and we should start doing so from a young age. Compliment them and praise them for their actions, but compliment and praise other adults for those things too. If a child or young person in your care sees you complimenting adults on their looks ('You look so pretty in that dress!'), they can internalize a narrative about what you value. I'm not saying that we should stop giving compliments relating to others' looks entirely, but if we shift a compliment to comment on their emotional well-being, we are reinforcing the importance of it to the child or young person observing the exchange. For instance, we can say instead, 'You look so happy in that dress!' or 'You look like you feel very strong today.'

2 Be aware of your own body talk

We can't change the culture relating to bodies and body dissatisfaction for children and young people if we don't practise what we preach. Children particularly respond more acutely to our actions than to our words, so if you tell them that they are perfect and special but then speak about your own body with derision, they will absorb that negativity. Similarly, children are more likely to copy what is demonstrated to them than they are to obey what they are told. Try not to use self-deprecating language or make self-deprecating jokes about your body. If you are trying to change your body (lose weight or get fit) it is helpful to make sure that you communicate the dissatisfaction you might feel in a way that focuses on your mental well-being and happiness rather than criticizing your body, that it is 'wrong' in some way.

3 Pass on how to spot fact and fiction in online marketing

It is very important that children and young people understand the difference between fact and fiction online – in particular, how things are presented for marketing reasons. Many children and young people internalize unrealistic expectations because of online marketing. Education is key to helping them know the difference.

When my son started using social media, we spent some time scrolling through his feed together so that I could point out the thinking behind the adverts he received. When he expressed interest in a popular body spray company, we discussed what the marketing people would want him to think and believe about the product to make him buy it. He understood that the advert was based on making him feel inadequate in attracting a partner, so he would buy the body spray, which would make him very attractive. That understanding added a little bit of resilience to his self-esteem.

When children or young people know that the content they see online is designed to manipulate their emotions, they can find it easier to notice and, hopefully, not fall for it and regulate their emotions accordingly.

4 Achieve regulation of emotions by getting physical

Since self-harm is a tool most young people use to regulate their emotions, it is helpful to introduce healthy ways to do that as alternatives.

Exercise is a great alternative as it can dispel the self-destructive or abusive cravings many young people might have. That is because exercise produces the same physical responses in the body as self-harm does – namely, adrenaline, serotonin, the heart racing, exertion and, ultimately, feeling alive.

When children and young people are so focused on their online presence and being, it is important and helpful for them to be reminded of their physical self in the real world. In a survey by the Mental Health Foundation,[14] young people were asked what substitute behaviours for self-harm were helpful, and they recommended:

- hitting a punchbag, to vent anger and frustration;
- having a good scream into a pillow or cushions or hitting pillows or cushions;
- getting outdoors for a fast walk;
- making lots of noise on musical instruments or banging pots and pans;
- all other forms of exercise.

Making children and young people aware of these tools can be very helpful. If they know that they have other ways and spaces in which they can express their anger, sadness and worry, then they are less likely to seek out relief via unhealthy means.

5 Suggest alternatives to self-harm

If young people are already engaging in self-harm, then they might struggle to stop and asking them to stop could cause them to withdraw from you. It is also important to accept that even if they did stop physically harming themselves, they would still have the urges and struggle to regulate their emotions in healthy ways.

So that they can move towards the healthy options, it can be helpful to suggest alternatives to self-harm. The best alternatives are actions that mimic the shock or physical impact of self-harm but without being harmful, such as:

- using a red felt-tip pen to draw on the skin as if cutting it – seeing the red, as a visual approximation of blood, can have a placebo effect;
- putting elastic bands on the wrists and flicking them when feeling the urge to self-harm – it provides a sharp shock of pain without the long-term damage;
- gripping an ice cube or taking a cold shower – the sudden cold provides the same shock to the system as pain;
- biting into something strongly flavoured – a sour lemon or a hot chilli.

Summary

In this chapter, we have discussed narratives relating to looks and how important it is for us, as adults, to model healthy attitudes to our own and others' bodies. In this way, we can help to boost the self-esteem of the children and young people around us so that they do not feel a need to turn to self-harm.

Self-reflection question

How would you characterize your own body talk? Do you often speak about yourself positively or negatively?

Self-reflection activity

Write down the compliments that mean the most to you when you receive them. How many of them are about your appearance? How many do you repeat to others? Consider how the compliments based on physical appearance could be changed and write down an alternative.

5

Depression in a dying world
Suicide and climate anxiety

Situation seems impossible to make it.
Hoping, dreaming,
Praying some day it will work out.
Uphill battle takes more strength
Than you can fathom.
Lily-Jo, song 'Unstoppable'

When I was 15, I was sure that the world was going to end. I grew up in a religious household and my parents spoke frequently about the end times. At Church and in the culture surrounding me, there was an unwavering certainty that soon, very soon, Christ would be returning and the Apocalypse would begin. When I entered my GCSE year at school, a part of me wondered, dismally, if there was any point in studying. By the time the exams came around, everything might be over. I'd seen videos explaining – in vivid, imaginative detail – the war to come, the ascension of the chosen and the golden gates of the new heaven. Revising photosynthesis seemed a bit irrelevant next to all that.

That time is what I am reminded of when I think about the burden and pressure placed on younger generations today by climate change. I remember that feeling of something dreadful and inevitable speeding towards me, completely out of my control. It doesn't surprise me, then, that 'climate anxiety', also known as 'eco-anxiety', have become more and more frequently used terms. It also doesn't surprise me that depression is on the rise among teenagers in the UK. An ONS study published in 2020 showed that nearly a third of women aged from 16 to 24 reported evidence of depression and anxiety, which is an increase of 5 per cent since the report produced five years previously.[1] We also know that, statistically, suicide rates among adolescents in the UK are increasing by 7.9 per cent per year.[2]

Talking about suicide and depression form a huge part of my job, both as a counsellor and as a mental health advocate, but what I want to talk about here are elements of both those things that seem largely specific to Gen Z: depression and suicidal thoughts brought about by fear of global destruction.

I am in no way suggesting that such thoughts are the only reason for the rise in suicide and depression in our youngest generations. The causes of mental ill health are always multifaceted and complex, but this type of thinking is perhaps most unfamiliar or alien to the generations that have come before. Why is the climate crisis having such a specific impact on mental health around the world?

Discussions about climate change can be contentious for some, so I want to start by saying that the practical tips at the end of this chapter are relevant to *any* person who is struggling with depression and suicidal thoughts or urges, not only those struggling with climate anxiety. My hope is that, even if we may not all see eye to eye about the planet, we can learn together how young people feel about the world they live in and how it is having an impact on their mental health. With that in mind, let's dive into exactly what we are talking about when we use the term 'climate anxiety'.

What is 'climate anxiety'?

In 2017, the American Psychiatric Association (APA) acknowledged climate anxiety, describing it as 'a chronic fear of environmental doom'.[3] It may seem absurd to say that a huge proportion of our young people are experiencing anxiety as a result of worrying about the end of the world, but the results of various studies support that assertion. For example, a survey carried out in America reported in 2021 that 83 per cent of Gen Z worry about the health of the planet and 75 per cent of those say that this worry has an impact on their mental health.[4] Those percentages may have been influenced by the fact that America, arguably, has seen more of the devastating impacts of climate change than has the UK, for instance – such as the wildfires in California and the West Coast heatwave of 2021. It is certainly true that climate anxiety is higher in places in the world where the impact of climate change is having a direct, measurable effect on infrastructure, services or health. When your home has been destroyed by a natural disaster due to changing weather patterns or someone you love has died due to unbearable, unexpected heat and the sudden pressure on emergency services, it is understandable that it will have an impact on both your physical and mental well-being. Studies have also shown that climate change has an effect on suicide rates, as there are more suicides reported during heatwaves and periods of unexpected heat.

Climate change can also exacerbate existing mental health problems, as natural disasters often have a knock-on effect to health providers. It is not surprising, then, that in a world where people are experiencing upheaval due to climate change, they develop anxiety as a result. Some people, however, experience climate anxiety even when they are not in a critical situation. This latter type of climate anxiety is the kind that plagues the vast majority of Gen Z in the Western world.

We might ask 'Why is that?' After all, if a child or young person is growing up in the relative safety of somewhere rural, for example, why are they so preoccupied with climate change that it drives them to despair?

The answer is that it is an anxiety born out of an uncertainty about the future, of living in a world where the timer for the planet was set, in 2019, by some climate scientists for 11 years' time.[5] For a teenager doing their GCSEs, that is a timescale which has the potential to rob them of their entire future. Not knowing whether or not it will come about is stressful and the 24-hour news cycle does nothing to alleviate that.

While knowledge is power and many young people are enlightened about the science of global warming, the glut of information they consume can lead to exacerbated feelings of hopelessness. That hopelesseness is due to a psychological effect called 'pseudo-inefficiency', which is when a person realizes the problem they are faced with has such a large scope, their small contribution to change begins to feel meaningless, so they don't know what to do and may end up doing nothing. It doesn't help that the media focuses on sensationalism and scandal rather than presenting solutions. Consequently, young people are paralysed between the fear that if they do not do something to save the world they are doomed and the hopelessness that nothing they do will have a significant impact.

Sarah Jaquette Ray, an environmental studies professor at Humboldt State University, describes how the Gen Z students in her class are 'traumatized' by climate disruption and frequently express their belief that the consumer sins of their parents will fall on their heads. She also describes how students become so depressed and filled with self-loathing that it leads them to destructive, almost suicidal behaviours. At its most extreme, climate anxiety can mean that students starve themselves in an effort to reduce their consumption.[6] It is not suicidal ideation as we would usually understand it – when a person longs for oblivion as a release from the pain of living – but, rather, when a person is so overwhelmed by guilt for being alive and a burden on the world that death is seen as a blessing for the world by being one less drain on its resources.

While that last way of thinking is an example of extreme nihilism, our research at the Lily-Jo Project echoes the global trends emerging on this topic. Our survey[7] found that 60 per cent of interviewees admitted thinking about the future of our planet made them feel anxious. When discussing climate change with a Gen Z student, they said:

I definitely worry about climate change more than the generations above us. We're taught about it in geography at school from primary school age, so we understand the facts and what's actually happening. We know that climate change is leading to a crisis. It makes me very anxious. I see it constantly. Even with the weather changing drastically in the UK, I know that's climate change. It scares me. I definitely feel threatened by it. I know it will be a life-or-death issue in my lifetime.

With such feelings of constant despair threatening to overtake them, it is not surprising to me as a mental health professional that climate anxiety can lead to depression and the possibility of suicidal ideation too. Why, when the mental health of so many young people is adversely affected by the effects of climate change, do older generations not worry so much and struggle to understand why the younger ones do?

Why does climate anxiety have a disproportionate effect on Gen Z and Gen Alpha?

When I heard the Gen Z student's response to our survey, honestly, I was quite surprised. I am concerned about climate change and, like any parent, I worry about the inheritance that global consumerism will leave for my children in the future. I try to be conscious – I have reusable bags and have cut down on dairy – but I have never really thought of climate change as a threat to my life. I looked into it, trying to understand why my children and others of their generation are so much more convinced of its life-threatening impact. After all, we have all the same facts, why do we not come to the same emotional conclusions? In short, why do they care so much more than I seem to?

I found out that it is due to something psychologists call 'psychological distance'. It means that a person can acknowledge climate change is real and is happening but maintain the belief that it is not a problem which has a direct impact on them. Research suggests that when we use words such as 'global' or 'climate', we are accidentally emphasizing the broader impacts rather than helping people to understand how personal it is. Those words encourage an emotional disconnect.

That is something I fully understand. As an adult, I have struggled to maintain a feeling of urgency about the climate crisis. Maybe I have been ignorant or sheltered – I know many people may say I am – but I also wonder if it is because I have already lived through believing that the world was going to end. I remember how that feels. Perhaps you do too.

Maybe it was the 9/11 or 7/7 terrorist attacks. Maybe it was the Troubles in Northern Ireland or maybe, like me, you grew up in a religious setting that enforced an apocalyptic world view. Like the baby boomers, who grew up with the adverts on TV telling them what to do in the event of a nuclear strike, and the silent generation, who grew up during the Blitz, Gen Z and Gen Alpha are growing up with climate change as the biggest threat on the doomsday clock. I don't say this to lessen the impact of climate change or to suggest that young people today are somehow foolish or overwrought in their concern – they are not. The science is definitely on their side. Besides, if you had told someone living in London in 1944 that it was silly to worry about a bomb falling on your house, that would have been absurd. Death was everywhere. Similarly, we cannot tell an entire generation growing up watching forest fires consume Australia and polar bears die of starvation that there is no way people they love will not be hurt by what's happening to the world. Humanity's past survival is not a promise of its future in the middle of a crisis. Yet that does not mean our older generations' perspective is valueless. In fact, I would suggest that it is vital. It gives us a key to compassion and understanding that we might otherwise have overlooked. We cannot guarantee our young people today that the world will not end, but we can treat them with compassion and support.

While treatment for climate anxiety is still evolving, the emerging consensus is that focusing on emotional resilience is vital in order to avoid the extreme depression which can lead to suicide. Resilience is what helps us to overcome a crisis and that is something the older generations can teach the younger generations. Those of us who have survived a global crisis in the past can offer resilience techniques that will help young people to shape their futures. In the practical guide that follows shortly, we will be looking at some resilience-building techniques to use to help when a person is at risk of falling into despair.

How can we have hope?

For young people, black-and-white thinking can block the potential for a more nuanced view of the world. That is because, for adolescents and young people under the age of 25, their brains are still developing. Social cognition and executive function in the brain are still being formed, which can lead to a type of thinking that prioritizes one point of view. On a practical level, that means a young person may be more likely to use phrases such as 'everyone hates me' or 'there's nothing we can do'. Because young people have access to so much information, it can be hard for them to see the other side of climate change – the hopeful side. How, then, can we have hope and help to give our young people hope?

Hope is a supremely personal thing. At the beginning of this chapter, I mentioned how a religious situation in my young life led me to feel less hopeful than previously, but I have also seen how enriching religious practice and community can be for individuals and families. There is hope to be found in the belief that there is something greater than we are. In Frances Ward's book, *Like There's No Tomorrow*, she wrestles with the questions climate change brings to people of faith. She suggests a few questions that I have found deeply powerful and which resonate with me:

> I came to ask myself a question that emerged as being fundamental: how can I be what I am meant to be, as I participate in the being of God? What of the fragile environments around? How do they have their being in God? How can human beings work with God to enable that being, rather than change, control or destroy?[54]

Whatever our personal feelings about God may be, those who are striving to redress the balance to deal with climate change all believe in the power of the world around us. It may even be considered sacred, beloved, worthy of protection. With that belief comes fear, because, for a lot of young people, they will see a world they love being destroyed. There is, however, a cycle of hope in there, too, which is that, if we believe the earth is powerful and holy and adaptive, we can believe in its ability to survive – we need only learn how to help it more effectively.

Faith is not something that we can or should ever press on a child or young person – it is deeply personal and a choice made in the soul, not the mind – yet hope is infinitely transferable. There are many times that I have been encouraged and even moved to grateful tears by the power of faith and the power of hope other people around me carry, people with vastly different religious upbringings and beliefs from mine. That is because hope, not blind optimism, is truly inspiring.

The thing I like most about the Frances Ward quote is that it is a call to action, to participate in hope rather than be crushed underneath grief – and we do have reason to hope. There is evidence that climate action is having an impact. There are more electric cars on the roads today than there were five years ago and, in 2019, more than six million people marched for climate action. In the World Wildlife Fund's (WWF) statement on the impact of climate action, it highlighted the importance of continued commitment to the cause:

> Collective power has extraordinary strength. Combining our voices to call for transformational climate action can influence political leaders, industries, and businesses – the top decision-makers on whom cutting carbon emissions depends.[9]

There is indeed hope in collective action. Helping our young people to realize that is paramount. I have always been particularly fond of the following quote from Martin

Luther King Jr, which seems very appropriate when we talk about the future: 'We must accept finite disappointment, but infinite hope.'[10] Our task as adults is to help our young people to learn how to accept the disappointments and losses they will experience due to climate change but also to rally and discover resources of infinite hope, perhaps through faith – be it faith in God, faith in the planet or faith in one another.

Practical guide to building emotional resilience – five top tips

Before we begin, let me remind you of a very important fact: *if you believe a child, young person (or anyone else) is at risk of taking their own life, please reach out for help.*

Before the 'Summary' at the end of this chapter, there is a list of resources to support you. Remember, you cannot be everything to a child or young person struggling with suicide. You cannot be the parent, carer, doctor *and* counsellor all at once – even if you are qualified! Get help from others, not only for their sake but also for your own.

1 Encourage fair and realistic thinking

Fair and realistic thinking is a tool we use to challenge unfounded assumptions that can lead to negative self-talk and depressive thoughts.

When children or young people experience worry, they often don't have the tools to challenge some of the assumptions that their mind is making. For instance, they may say, 'I feel depressed because the world is ending and we're all going to die.' They understand that to be true, as it is based on their worry about climate change, which is based on scientific fact, but they have not examined fully the statements their mind has accepted in order to reach that point. They have assumed that, because the climate change situation looks dire, their own death is imminent. To take another example, a depressed young person may say, 'Everybody hates me because I'm so depressed.'

Both examples show how our assumptions can affect our mood. Fair and realistic thinking challenges those assumptions. You can put it into practice by encouraging the child or young person to challenge their thinking. When they present a catastrophizing thought or negative assumption, try to ask them or direct them to ask themselves, 'What if I'm wrong?' or 'What evidence do I have to support that?' The act of self-enquiry will give the child or young person some separation from their thoughts and allow them to analyse those thoughts rationally.

Fair and realistic thinking reduces panic and despair but also encourages the development of mental resilience for the future.

2 Keep them connected to the truth

Emotional resilience is helped by positive affirmations of truth. As we identified before, the 24-hour news cycle has turned truth into a fickle thing. Facts can be unhelpful when people are overwhelmed or filled with despair, but positive affirmations of emotional truth can be helpful, especially when they focus on the control individuals have over their own lives.

Despair makes a person feel helpless, so if a child or young person is overwhelmed by climate anxiety affirmations, try different affirmations, such as 'my choices matter' and 'I can make a difference.' Such statements focus on personal responsibility without being too oppressive. Other positive statements that can help when someone has succumbed to despair are:

- 'I am worthy of life.'
- 'I have value.'
- 'The future is not hopeless.'

Allowing children or young people to choose their own affirmations helps to reinforce that feeling of taking back control, which is important for developing resilience. When people believe that they have control over themselves, it can help them to prepare emotionally for situations that are outside their control.

3 Help them to stay in the present

In crisis situations, when people feel utterly out of control, it can be helpful to get them to connect with the present. Similarly, if a child or young person is struggling with despair or suicidal thoughts and cannot fathom a future for themselves, it can be difficult to get them to focus on what comes next without them experiencing feelings of panic or terror. In those cases, try to help the child or young person to live in the moment.

At the Lily-Jo Project, we use 'mindful moment' practices. Our favourite is 'three, five breathing', to help ground the body in the moment and stop the mind from cycling too rapidly. To do this, the child or young person first breathes in for a count of three and out for a count of five, then slowly increases the counts to 'four, six' and then 'five, seven' breathing, if they feel calm enough. The child or young person can either focus on the counting or may respond well to positive visualization of a safe space. One of our staff members at the Lily-Jo Project visualizes a zoo, where she spent a lot of time during her childhood!

Staying in the present is a useful resilience tool for when a child or young person is feeling overwhelmed.

4 Make a safe space for sharing

Choosing or creating a space that children or young people view as safe in which to share things is very valuable as it teaches them that they can build their resilience by means of their own actions. I like to think of it as teaching them 'emotional fort building'. It allows them to see that, when they are overwhelmed, they can make their own space and find their own people who make them feel safe. Making yourself part of that safe space can benefit parent–child bonding as well. Don't underestimate the impact of a non-judgemental, kind presence, even if a child or young person doesn't speak at first or seems uncomfortable.

Don't underestimate either the relief that can be gained from appropriate physical contact. Tight hugs can be helpful in relieving anxiety as, when we hug, the body releases oxytocin, which lightens our mood. Studies with infants show that there is a perfect 'tightness' for a hug – not too weak nor too constricting – that lowers the heart rate and reduces anxiety.

Let yourself be guided by the child or young person as to what seems appropriate. Try giving a firm hug, holding it for at least 20 seconds, but loosen or let go if they seem uncomfortable. If it is not appropriate for physical contact to be made or the child or young person is reticent, you might consider products that provide a similar feeling, such as weighted blankets, to provide the assurance without the touching.

5 Use reflective language

Resilience is built by means of a process of sharing what is truly going on inside. When a child or young person learns that they can find relief in communication, then they are on the path away from self-destruction.

When a child or young person is very depressed or suicidal, however, such a process is not always possible in the same way, as conversation with them can be very difficult. That is because often, when they are struggling, they find it hard to communicate, especially with someone they know and especially a parent, because they are worried about how the darkness of their thoughts will be perceived. For that reason, it is very important to think about how you listen and respond.

If a child or young person receives a verbal or non-verbal cue that you are shocked or distressed by their words, it is possible that they could interpret it as rejection or condemnation. This can prompt them to hide things and retreat. When a child or young person expresses that they feel very depressed or suicidal, that they think about hurting themselves or say things like, 'I wish I didn't exist', try to use reflective language in the following way.

- Listen carefully, without judgement or overt physical reactions.
- Encourage them to talk if they seem to struggle to do so by using positive but relaxed sentences, such as, 'I don't know what you're going through but I would like to try to understand.'
- Repeat their words back to them rather than interpret them. For instance, if a child or young person says, 'I wish I had never been born', try saying, 'Can you tell me more about wishing you had never been born?', rather than saying, 'Tell me why you're suicidal.' When we repeat their words and phrases, we are showing them that we have listened and we are accepting their narrative, rather than trying to enforce our own.
- Don't rationalize or try to 'fix things'. Offering solutions

can often be interpreted as criticism or an attempt to dismiss the person's thoughts and feelings. You could ask instead, 'What do you think may help today?' or 'What could I do that might make you feel a bit better today?' That way, the child or young person suffering feels that they are being heard, but also that they are maintaining control.

• Express your gratitude for their openness and honesty. It can be tempting to tell a child or young person that they would be missed if they died, that you would be lost without them, but for someone who is feeling suicidal, that can make them feel emotionally manipulated or lead them to feel grief for the pain they are causing others. Instead, tell them that you are proud of/grateful to them for being so honest and praise their bravery in being open about what's happening. It helps to increase positive associations with communicating their feelings.

Supporting someone who is suicidal – resources

If you are reading this book and someone in your life is suicidal or has expressed suicidal feelings, please remember that you are not alone. It can be easy to slip into a feeling of responsibility, especially if the person in question is a family member or child, as though you are solely responsible for keeping that person alive, but it is not true.

You cannot and should not control every aspect of the person's behaviour – it is both unhealthy for you and not conducive to that person's healing. One of the hardest things about loving or caring for someone who is suicidal is having to accept and embrace the fact that the other person is in control, not you. All you can do is be a good friend, parent, carer or listener. You can learn more about how to do that by looking at the resources below, but I also recommend speaking to Samaritans, as its volunteers have a wealth of experience and can guide you through this. Call them on 116 123 or email them at <jo@samaritans.org>.

If someone in your care or someone you care about confides that they are presently trying to end their life or you fear that they are in imminent danger of causing themselves harm, please call the emergency services.

Online resources to support people having suicidal thoughts

Rethink Mental Illness
'Suicidal thoughts – how to support someone' factsheet, advice and information are available at:
<www.rethink.org/advice-and-information/carers
-hub/suicidal-thoughts-how-to-support-someone>
Tel.: 0808 801 0525
Email: advice@rethink.org

Mind
Offers information and support. See 'Supporting someone who feels suicidal' at:
<www.mind.org.uk/information-support/helping -someone-else/supporting-someone-who-feels -suicidal/about-suicidal-feelings>
Tel.: 0300 123 3393 (Infoline)
Email: <info@mind.org.uk>

Young Minds
Provides support for young people, parents and those who work with young people. See 'A guide for parents: suicidal thoughts' at:
<https://youngminds.org.uk/find-help/for-parents /parents-guide-to-support-a-z/parents-guide-to -support-suicidal-thoughts>
Tel.: 0808 802 5544 (parents' helpline)
Email and webchat: select chat icon on website

Papyrus
Working to prevent young suicide. Visit the website for help and advice resources at:
<www.papyrus-uk.org>
Tel.: 0800 068 4141 (Hopeline – suicide prevention helpline)
Email: <pat@papyrus-uk.org>

Summary

In this chapter, we discussed climate anxiety and how the attitudes of children and young people towards climate change and environmental questions can be very different from those of older adults, even leading to suicidal thoughts. Practical advice and resources are given on how to tackle such thoughts and build emotional resilience.

Self-reflection question

Consider your attitudes towards climate change. What reasons can you imagine there would be for a young person to be driven to feelings of hopelessness because of climate change?

Self-reflection activity

In this chapter, we discussed how to support a young person struggling with thoughts of suicide. One of the tips was to create a safe space in which a child or young person could feel safe enough to open up. Write down either details of safe spaces that you feel you have created for the children or young people in your care or one you would like to create for them.

6

Global grief

Political turbulence and understanding grief

And the look upon your face
And the moment you can't replace
Will someone erase this pain
And restore my innocence?
Lily-Jo, song 'Bring me back'

During the time I spent writing this book, we all experienced several moments of global grief. Moments that, in years to come, we will be asked where we were when we heard the news that rocked the world, causing unprecedented political fallout. In 2022, Russia began its war with Ukraine, and 19 children were killed in a mass shooting in south Texas. In 2021, Sarah Everard was murdered in London by a policeman, and in Washington, rioters stormed Capitol Hill. In 2020, despite the pandemic, one of the biggest questions on everyone's lips was, 'Did you hear about George Floyd?'

Floyd died at the hands of the police in Minneapolis in May 2020, suffocated to death after an officer applied pressure to his neck for nearly ten minutes (originally thought to be eight minutes 46 seconds). His death was the catalyst for a global anti-police violence and racism movement that spread throughout the world like wildfire, along with the devastating footage of his death.

I watched him die on Instagram, staring at my phone in complete shock. There, among the normal dog pictures and reels of people's sourdough starters, was the murder of a man. I couldn't believe what was happening, what I was witnessing. I've seen many significant moments online, but never anything like that.

As so many other parents did, I worried about my children seeing it – that they might stumble across such a traumatic event on their phone of all places. No parent wants their child, whatever age, to witness a murder. I also worried about how we would talk about it. I had talked about race a little with my eldest child, since he has encountered some unpleasant racial assumptions made about him at school, but nothing on such a scale.

I am blessed, and my children are blessed, that we live in a part of the UK where racial diversity is not only tolerated but also celebrated. We've been safe. My children have been given no reason to fear the police because of the colour of their skin. I watched what happened in Minneapolis and I worried that would change for them. Things had changed for me. People were suddenly asking me about my perspective as a mixed-race person and schools were asking for mental health resources relating to racism. Those were good things, but there were difficult things, too, and I worried about what impacts they would have on the lives of my children. I worried that, just as suddenly, I was feeling unsafe in the world as a person of colour, in a way I never had before, and they would feel unsafe as well.

Then there was anger. Sad, complicated rage that something like that had happened, that I lived in a world like this. He could have been my grandad, my dad or my brother. Somehow, even though I never met George Floyd, I felt strong anger that was personal. Anger for my relatives, for everyone who looks like me who has struggled, anger for my children. I grieved for George Floyd, for his family, for how racism had ruined their lives and how it was changing my children's lives. What happened in Minneapolis was so far away from my life in Manchester, in the UK, but, still, I grieved. I grieved again in 2021 when Sarah Everard was murdered in London, I grieved for myself and for my daughter and all the other women around the world who are still so much more vulnerable than we should be. I grieved again in 2022, when 19 children were shot to death in their school. I grieved for those children who were gone and I grieved for those who had survived but would be living in a different reality – one where the safe places were not safe any more.

Grief is such a complicated emotion, one that we all feel differently. Though it follows basic principles that we can anticipate (the five stages of grief), it is also possible to grieve for people we have never met. That is what I mean when I speak about 'global grief'. Events such as the ones I have mentioned are times in world history when people from all different nations come together to grieve for someone they didn't know personally. A recent example would be the death of Queen Elizabeth II in September 2022. In counselling, we call experiences like these 'existential touchstones'. Emotional moments when we see grief in the world, unconnected with our own personal experience, but we experience it as though it were our own.

Older examples of global grief might be the death of Diana, Princess of Wales, or even the terrorist attacks on the World Trade Center in New York in 2001. For me, 9/11 was my first instance of global grief, the first time a large-scale tragedy had a huge emotional impact on me. It was the first time I realized that I was mourning for people I had never met, feeling their grief and sadness. Although I didn't understand it at the time, it was also connected to my own fears and worries about a world that I perceived to be entirely out of my control.

Moments of global grief can be formative for children and young people, particularly those who now have unprecedented levels of access to them. When 9/11 took place, the most exposure I had to the event was what I saw in the BBC news broadcasts and read in the newspapers. Today's children and young people experience global grief very differently. They can hear the stories of people close to the epicentre of the trauma, they can listen to them and experience them over and over again online. It is no wonder that they experience high levels of anger and distress about the world they live in. They can watch a man being murdered in a video, listen to the last calls made by children from a school during 9/11 on TikTok. Their exposure is so much greater than mine was when I was growing up.

In this chapter, we are going to be looking at how to support children and young people who are struggling with living in overwhelming political climates and fighting to process their grief in healthy ways. The methods I propose can also be used to support those who are grieving a more personal loss, however. First, though, let's look at global grief and why it has such an impact on children and young people today.

Living a teenage life today is exhausting

Many times so far in this book I have pointed out how the world in which children and young people are growing up is radically different from the one millennials, Gen X or baby boomers grew up in. It is really important, however, that we realize how the world, as it is currently, is changing how young people manage their emotions. In her investigative article 'Teen depression and anxiety: Why the kids are not alright', Susanna Schrobsdorff examined why teenagers in Gen Z are struggling so much with their mental health. In her in-depth analysis of the culture that has formed Gen Z (and is currently forming Gen Alpha), she pointed out that political turbulence has been incredibly significant in that process:

They are the post-9/11 generation, raised in an era of economic and national insecurity. They've never known a time when terrorism and school shoot-ings weren't the norm. They grew up watching their parents weather a severe recession, and, perhaps most important, they hit puberty at a time when technology and social media were transforming society . . . being a teenager today is a draining full-time job that includes doing schoolwork, managing a social-media identity and fretting about career, climate change, sexism, racism – you name it . . . It's exhausting.[1]

While many of those things may be social and personal stressors that we all remember from when we grew up (after all, school and career fears were factors for me too!), the digital *hyperconnectedness* – which didn't exist at all then but is so prominent now – means Gen Z are feeling things like sexism and racism in ways that produce extreme results.

Research into the impact of this digital hyperconnectedness has shown that young people react to incidents thousands of miles away as though they were happening to people they know intimately. They have access to everything – if a suicide happens on the other side of the world, a young person might well hear about it on social media before any adults do.[2] They are also more aware of violence and, just as social media allows young people to witness such acts of violence, it also allows them to see the patterns. Hashtags mean they know that what might have been considered isolated incidents are, in fact, not. The #BlackLivesMatter and #MeToo and #TransLivesMatter hashtags help young people to understand on a deeper level that injustice is not only systematic and everywhere but also that they can take an active role in calling it out.[3] When we interviewed secondary school students about their understanding of the Internet and politics,[4] they connected it immediately to their own activism. A student named G said:

> The Internet has become such a vast space over the last two years. There is much more awareness online and information spreads a lot easier. Something negative, a viral movement or viral moment like George Floyd's murder, it gets passed around because people want to know and help and raise awareness. That's how I found out about Black Lives Matter.

That proactive instinct is one of the most admirable things about our young people – they are amazing. It can, however, also make them more vulnerable to grief.

The cost of being the instigation generation

Statistically, Gen Z are more political than any of the generations that came before them. They are more likely to let their politics influence their purchasing decisions – something online retailers have become attuned to, changing their slogans and branding to appeal to these eco-conscious, socially aware buyers. Their politics don't stop with what they buy either.

They are organizers and instigators. In 2020, the Black Lives Matter (BLM) march in Manchester, with more than 15,000 people taking part, was organized purely online by a 19-year-old student. The anti-gun violence movement March For Our Lives in the USA was founded by students who survived the Parkland school shooting in Florida. Gen Z are not content with raising awareness; they desire action. When we asked G, a year 11 student who is an anti-bullying ambassador at their school about why Gen Z is so politically invested, they had this to say:

> We care about politics because we understand what it is. We understand how it can affect people. If it can affect them negatively, then we want to fight to see if it can be corrected.

They are not only willing to fight to correct injustices but they are also willing to take risks. According to Dana Fisher, author of *American Resistance* (Columbia University Press, 2019), young people are more likely than those aged over 30 to be involved in protests as well as being more likely than them to accept the risk that the protests will become violent.[5] We could assume this is the pride or innocence of youth, them believing they are invincible in some way, but research shows that, in fact, it is to do with Gen Z's emotional range. John Della Volpe, from Harvard Kennedy School's Institute of Politics, has pointed out that the variety of what Gen Z experience in the world around them has had an emotional impact on them:

They've had friends, families, relationships with people who have been different from you based on whatever the difference is: socioeconomic, gender identity, and therefore, they've noticed that those friends and family members, even acquaintances are really no different than you as a generation. That is part of the reason they've been filled with so much empathy.[6]

That empathy and their access to social media allow Gen Z to cross boundaries that previously would have been unreasonable. For example, the March For Our Lives movement was begun by mostly white teenagers in Florida, yet they made the conscious effort to connect with members of the Black Lives Matter (BLM) movement.[7] We saw a similar thing happen in Manchester, when those who had marched for BLM in 2020 went on to march at the protest about violence against women in 2021 after the murder of Sarah Everard. The capacity young people have for extraordinary empathy has formed them into political instigators, with the capability to change the world. It is truly one of the best things about my work with young people, seeing them devote themselves so passionately to bringing about a better future. I have, however, also seen how that passion can turn to grief, because having such huge empathy means that they are also capable of feeling profound grief.

I am so proud that my children are members of such empathetic, politically active, socially aware young generations. I look at them and I am amazed by their tenderness, acceptance and overwhelming sense of justice. I would never suggest that they should be less of any of those things; I would never try to take away what makes them so unique and wonderful. That is why it is important not to dismiss their global grief when they feel it. The grief they feel in solidarity with young people like them supporting causes or highlighting issues in marches around the world is just as valid and potentially painful as the grief they would feel if those causes or issues were affecting someone they knew at school.

There are many tools we use to combat grief. I have assembled some that I have used to help my clients, whether it is the result of a trauma in their close community or something that has happened far away to cause global grief.

Practical guide to dealing with grief – five top tips

1 Choose your words carefully

Grief can come at us at the strangest moments. We often expect grief when a person dies, but it can also be brought on by other events – when someone has lost their job, been diagnosed with a disease, lost a pet, witnessed a trauma or is processing global grief. Due to the variety of causes, it is very important not to make assumptions about the child or young person's grief. It is unhelpful to say things like:

- 'Everything happens for a reason.'
- 'It's God's will.'
- 'I know how you feel.'
- 'Be strong.'

Such phrases are unhelpful because they can be perceived as belittling, condescending or dismissive. Language that focuses instead on the experience of the individual, validates their feelings and makes them feel listened to is often well received. Examples of good things to say are:

- 'I am so sorry for your loss.'
- 'I am here to help in any way I can.'
- 'I am just a phone call away.'
- 'My favourite memory of your loved one is . . .'

Simply being with the person who is grieving and saying nothing at all can be incredibly comforting. If you don't know what to say, therefore, offer to literally 'be there' for them.

2 Help them to deal with their anger

With grief, inevitably there is often a lot of anger and distress. A person may express their disbelief that the trauma happened and anger that it happened to them.

With a young person, it can help to guide them to express their anger in constructive ways. One of the things I often suggest to clients is writing an anger letter. Here is an example of a plan for one that I often use.

Step 1 Grab a piece of paper and start with 'Dear X'.

Step 2 Express all your thoughts and feelings here. Use capitals, get everything that's inside out and on to the page.

Step 3 Take a moment to think about what you feel. Reflect on what has been written and let those words and the truth of them sink in.

Step 4 Write, 'However, I now choose to . . .'. That is the point when you decide what you want to do or to happen next. For example, 'I now choose to call the police/forgive/focus on remembering the good times/ take action or get involved in a group working towards making sure something like that never happens again.'

Step 5 Choose what you would like to do with the letter. Shred it, burn it, keep it. Anger letters are not for sending, they are for our own personal reflection.

Step 5 Notice how you feel. What impact has writing the letter had on your feelings? Do you feel relieved? Raw? Sad? Grateful?

Most people feel like a weight has been lifted after completing an anger letter. Once this process is complete, it is then a good idea to encourage your young person to change the focus of their attention and do something that they enjoy.

3 Help them to find a way to mourn

As human beings, we often need rituals to help us to process grief. That is why we find funerals therapeutic and cathartic. If a funeral is not an option, though, it can be helpful to find some other outlet for their mourning.

Times of global grief show how such alternative rituals may be developed. For instance, the mural of George Floyd painted in Manchester in the wake of his death was visited by thousands of people, many placing candles and cards by it to express their grief. Children and young people find this approach particularly helpful, as it gives them access to a process that can help them to understand their grief, especially for instances of global grief. In a few schools we have worked with, staff have created an annual ritual to memorialize the Manchester Arena bombing. The children release balloons, perform dance or music, and spend some time in silence, reflecting on the event. They find it a helpful way to express their feelings within a structured environment.

Writing letters, making cards or memorial videos, or lighting candles are all examples of mourning rituals that can help children and young people to process their grief.

4 Enable them to put grief aside at times

Grief can overwhelm every part of life. For a child or young person, that might reveal itself in a growing lack of interest in school or activities, or an increase in seeking isolation.

Something that can be helpful is to find a way to allow a child or young person to compartmentalize their grief, so they can enjoy other parts of their life without feeling guilty about doing so. Often, children and young people worry that if they are not grieving all the time, they are somehow dishonouring the memories they have. Creating a memory box, with significant items relating to a death or other traumatic event, can provide a fixed space and time when they can grieve for it. Then, when they are not spending time looking at their memory box, they can release themselves to pursue happiness again.

5 Offer ideas for a gratitude practice

At a certain stage in the grieving process, once someone has begun to process their anger and found ways to memorialize the person who has died or done whatever feels appropriate for them, it can be helpful to introduce a daily gratitude practice.

Adults may choose to do this in the form of daily affirmations or a gratitude journal, and those options are helpful for young people, too, but they often react well to an external, verbal process that encourages them to be comfortable sharing their emotions with others. At the Lily-Jo Project, we often start our regular clubs or lessons with a mental health check-in or gratitude practice. We go around the group and ask the children or young people to share one thing that they are grateful for. It gives us a chance to monitor their mental health but also gets the children or young people into the habit of monitoring their own well-being and noticing their emotions. Reminding them that there are things to be grateful for can help to provide balance for the grief they are feeling.

Summary

In this chapter, we discussed political turbulence and coping with grief. We also established the necessity of understanding the power instances of global grief have over young people, and even children.

Self-reflection question

Have you ever experienced an instance of global grief that had a significant impact on you? What was it?

Self-reflection activity

It is helpful when offering guidance to children and young people about activities to process grief if you have some experience of using them yourself. Take some time to try one – either writing an anger letter or a gratitude list. Consider carefully how the activity makes you feel afterwards and note down those feelings. Then, when recommending the activity, you can genuinely share your own experiences of using it.

7

Fear in the fluid generation
Mental health and being LGBTQ+

Watching you grow
From the shadows
Nothing can stop you no matter what tries to
Get in your way.
You'll have your day
So follow your happiness.
Lily-Jo, song 'Diamond'

In 2022, the debut series of *Heartstopper*, a romance between two boys who meet at school, premiered on Netflix. The critics gave it a score of 100 per cent in their review on the entertainment recommendation site Rotten Tomatoes,[1] which is very rare these days and proof that positive lesbian, gay, bisexual, transgender, queer/questioning and others (LGBTQ+) content is here to stay. From working in schools, I know how powerful the graphic novels by Alice Oseman (on which the programme is based) are for young people and many of them are happy to see themselves and their friends represented so positively onscreen.

In the story, Charlie Spring and Nick Nelson navigate coming out in their teenage years and beginning a new relationship. They struggle with homophobia and biphobia all around them, at school and sometimes at home, and that, quite naturally, has a knock-on effect on their mental health. What *Heartstopper* made me think of, however, is just how much fear young LGBTQ+ people often have to deal with in the world.

Charlie Spring has difficulties arising from social anxiety, due to a history of being bullied because he is gay. Unfortunately, Charlie's experience is not unique. People who identify as LGBTQ+ are disproportionately affected by mental health problems. A study carried out by Youth Chances showed that 52 per cent of LGBTQ+ people reported self-harming, compared to 35 per cent of non-LGBTQ+ people, and 44 per cent of LGBTQ+ respondents reported suicidal thoughts, compared to 26 per cent of non-LGBTQ+ respondents.[2] The results of the study reflect a global trend, as has also been shown in the Trevor Project's 2022 national survey on young people's mental health, which revealed that a startling proportion of LGBTQ+ teenagers (aged from 13 to 17) had considered attempting suicide in the past year: *50 per cent*.[66] It is a horribly high percentage, especially when the survey also found that 18 per cent of young LGBTQ+ people had attempted suicide. That is more than twice the rate of suicide attempts among teenagers in the USA, which is 9 per cent. Those are shocking statistics and should, rightly, prompt us to take action.

When I read those statistics, one question alone came to mind: '*Why?*' After all, from my perspective as a straight person, it seems as though we are living in an age where

LGBTQ+ issues are becoming more and more mainstream, especially when compared to how it was when I grew up. Young people's attitudes now are radically different from when I was at school, with half of Gen Z believing that traditional gender roles and labels relating to the binary genders alone are outdated.[4] That kind of thinking is reflected in the way companies advertise today, and I definitely notice more representation of gender-neutral or fluid people in advertising. The world is changing, into a place where Netflix viewers streamed a queer love story between two British teenage boys for almost 24 million hours in the week between 25 April and 1 May,[5] and where Jake Daniels, the Blackpool FC forward, in 2022 became the first active British footballer to come out publicly.[6] Why, then, are young LGBTQ+ people struggling so much?

I have been privileged to hear the stories of LGBTQ+ people in my team and those of young people in schools and what I have learnt from their experiences has helped me to understand some of the problems that young LGBTQ+ people face today. It has made me realize that, in truth, feeling afraid and experiencing mental health problems is not only a natural human response to the trauma many people experience but also, perhaps, to be expected. Let's look at the facts together.

Hate breeds fear

I remember very clearly the attack on Pulse nightclub in Orlando in 2016, where 49 people were killed and 53 people were injured when a 29-year-old man committed a hate crime against the LGBTQ+ community. I remember how moving it was to see images of people queuing for hours to donate blood afterwards, but what I shall never forget are the text messages that were published online – those last conversations between the victims and their loved ones, many between parents and young people under the age of 25. The youngest victim was only 18 years old.[7] They really reinforced a truth for me, that the victims of hate crimes against LGBTQ+ people can be and often are young people.

Studies have shown that, since 2014, homophobic hate crime reports have tripled in the UK, and transphobic hate crimes have quadrupled.[8] During the pandemic, it became even worse, as LGBTQ+ people were blamed by some people for COVID-19. Speaking to the charity EachOther, Leni Morris, who is Chief Executive of Galop, an LGBTQ+ charity, said:

> this was either because the pandemic was seen as a punishment for our existence, or because of our community's association with the HIV/AIDS pandemic, and a notion that LGBTQ+ people were somehow at the root of this pandemic.[9]

Yet, despite the rise in incidents, government figures show that 90 per cent of this type of hate crime goes unreported, with younger LGBTQ+ people being particularly averse to going to the police.[10]

The reasons given for their fear of the police are legion, their discomfort based on not only what they have experienced in their own lives but also what they have seen happen in the lives of others or online. An article published in the Notre Dame Catholic Sixth Form College's student newspaper in Leeds listed some reasons given by young LGBTQ+ people in a survey of their peers:

- lack of trust;
- feeling unsafe around the police due to a history of their racism towards people who are not white;
- the police have a history of mistreating queer people;
- regarding the participants' personal views of how hate crime reports from queer and trans persons were being handled by the police, they thought that the police had not been educated sufficiently about the issues and were dismissive of the reports.[11]

Given that we know there is a connection between experiencing a hate crime or hate-based violence and PTSD, it is little wonder that so many young LGBTQ+ people struggle with mental ill health. A study conducted by the International Society for Traumatic Stress Studies into PTSD symptoms among young LGBTQ+ people revealed that they had higher PTSD scores than young straight people who have experienced hate crimes.[12] Further, the study showed that it is not hate crimes alone that affect levels of PTSD and mental health but also:

The impact of prejudice and discrimination may extend beyond the trauma routinely associated with criminal victimization, challenging the survivor's sense of self.[13]

For many young LGBTQ+ people, prejudice and discrimination come in the form of bullying, whether at school or in the community, though it is not always violent. If we take the example presented to us in the TV show *Heartstopper*, Charlie experiences casual prejudice from his peers and sexual aggression. That type of bullying is experienced by 1 in 3 bisexual young people, 57 per cent of non-binary people, 80 per cent of disabled young people, 79 per cent of LGBTQ+ people of colour and nearly half of all LGBTQ+ young people.[14]

In my role as a counsellor, I see many people who are still carrying the wounds of childhood in their adult lives and, as mentioned in earlier chapters, bullying of any kind can have various negative effects on a person's mental well-being. Is it any wonder, then, when facing all this, that so many young LGBTQ+ people struggle with mental ill health? There is an additional challenge facing young LGBTQ+ people today, however: accessing appropriate mental health care.

Fear breeds silence

For many of my adult friends who identify as LGBTQ+, accessing adequate health care, both mental and physical, is a significant battle. Many of them have had negative experiences with a health care professional and the national statistics from Stonewall echo what they have found. Stonewall's study showed that:

- almost one in four patients (23 per cent) had witnessed negative remarks about LGBTQ+ people being made by health care staff while accessing services;
- one in seven LGBTQ+ people (14 per cent) said that they have avoided treatment altogether for fear of the discrimination they may face;
- of those who did seek support, one in eight (13 per cent) have experienced some form of unequal treatment from health care staff because they're LGBTQ+;
- a quarter of LGBTQ+ people (25 per cent) faced a lack of understanding of their specific health needs – a figure that rises to 62 per cent for trans patients.[15]

Another difficulty LGBTQ+ people face is that services specifically designed to support their mental health are horrendously oversubscribed and underfunded, and that is particularly true for young LGBTQ+ people. A YouGov report with Stonewall revealed that one in ten (10 per cent) of health and social care practitioners are not confident in their ability to understand and meet the specific needs of lesbian, gay or bisexual patients and service users. A quarter (24 per cent) are not confident in their ability to respond to the specific care needs of trans patients and service users.[16]

Such a lack of confidence means that many LGBTQ+ people rely on charities rather than the NHS to provide them with the support they need. The result of this is that, for many of my friends and other LGBTQ+ people, GPs and hospitals do not feel like safe spaces or places in which they will be taken seriously, treated well or respected. Now, for children or young people, such feelings are amplified, especially when we remember that young people are the least likely to come forward when they have experienced a hate crime that might cause a significant mental health trauma. Besides that, young people often feel as though they don't have anyone to confide in who could help. More than half young LGBTQ+ people don't feel as though there is an adult at school or college who they can confide in and three in five say that they don't have an adult they can speak to at home either.[17]

Ultimately, I feel the burden of those statistics. If either of my children ever comes out to me, I want them to feel safe enough to seek help at school and to trust me enough to open up at home. In addition to that, as the founder of a mental health charity, I want to help build a world where everyone has access to someone to talk to about their mental health and never feels cut off from that help because of their gender identity or sexuality. I've come to the conclusion that young LGBTQ+ people are in need of adults who they feel will not simply tolerate them but also celebrate them and advocate for them.

How can we help young LGBTQ+ people to feel supported to ensure their mental well-being? How can we encourage them to feel safe? How can we be good allies?

Practical guide to breaking the silence and being an ally to LGBTQ+ young people – five top tips

Before we begin, I want to speak directly to any parents, carers or adults in positions of responsibility for young people who are feeling overwhelmed by the challenge of supporting young LGBTQ+ people. I want you to know that I understand how you feel. It can seem daunting, especially if you are not LGBTQ+ or do not have LGBTQ+ friends to talk to about it. I understand that sometimes the desire to avoid saying the wrong thing can overwhelm our desire to help and we can end up saying nothing.

I think it is really important for us to remember that we are all flawed human beings and sometimes we are going to get things wrong. Sometimes we might use the wrong word and sometimes we might reveal the limits of our knowledge, but what I have learnt is that saying a simple, 'I'm sorry, I didn't know that' goes a long way.

We can't promise that we will be perfect, but we can promise to be as loving and respectful as we possibly can and learn from our mistakes. Here are some tips to help break the silence so you can be a good ally to young LGBTQ+ people.

1 Know your resources

Research is important. It's totally understandable that there may be gaps in your knowledge about the mental health challenges and lives of young LGBTQ+ people – after all, historically, their stories have been suppressed or stereotyped in mainstream media, and education about LGBTQ+ rights and welfare is still not part of formal curriculums in many schools and countries around the world.

The truth is that every LGBTQ+ person is different, just as every young person is unique, and they each come with their own cultural background to navigate. For example, the types of experiences a young LGBTQ+ person in a diverse urban community will have had may be wildly different from those of a young LGBTQ+ person growing up in a more conservative rural community or in your community, whatever that may be. It's important to learn as much as you can about the young person who needs your support. There are many websites that can help, but I recommend Mind (<www.mind.org.uk>) as a good place to start, and Stonewall (<www.stonewall.org.uk>).

2 Listen

Once you have done your research, it can be really tempting to forge straight ahead and 'download' all the information you have found out on to the child or young person, as though you are trying to prove that you are accepting of them! That can make the child or young person feel awkward. It is better, by far, to simply listen to them.

Don't make assumptions about their sexuality based on your knowledge – wait for them to share their identity with you in their own time. Coming out to you or talking about their sexuality without being asked or prompted is a sign that the young person trusts you and thinks of you as 'safe' on some level, as they are trusting you with that information. If you corner the young person into answering or they feel pressured by your questions, it will have the opposite of the desired effect. It's the difference between sharing a secret and having a secret pried out of you. Only one is a gift and a sign of trust.

3 Pronouns

Pronouns are important. The Trevor Project's national survey showed that transgender and non-binary young people who reported having their pronouns respected by all the people they lived with attempted suicide at half the rate that those who did not have their pronouns respected by those they lived with.[18] For that reason alone, I always endorse it. It is such a simple way to help a young person to feel loved and valued and, possibly, save their life.

One of the easiest ways to approach pronouns if you are unsure is to use your own pronouns when you introduce yourself. For instance, 'My name is Lily-Jo and my pronouns are she/her. Would you like to tell me your name and pronouns?' When you make a mistake, correct yourself and simply move on. Don't make a big deal of your mistake with profuse apologies and explanations – that is only likely to make the young person uncomfortable. If you are struggling with pronouns, I suggest practising using their correct pronouns when you talk about that young person with other people or when you think of them inside your head.

4 Creating a safe space

Creating a safe space is not always about a physical space; it's about reassuring the child or young person that you will not tolerate discrimination when you encounter it, you are increasing the visibility of LGBTQ+ people and you will help them to stay safe.

As noted before, children and young people are always watching us! If they see that you allow a homophobic joke to go unchecked, they will mentally log that it is not safe for them to be themselves around you. If, instead, they see that you call out discrimination in your home, youth group or classroom, then they will pick up the message that you will not hurt them in the way that others may have done. If they hear you talk about an openly gay musician or recommend books or TV shows with LGBTQ+ themes, then they can be encouraged by that. These things signal acceptance, saying, 'I have accepted the work of this artist and I will accept you too.' If you also communicate with children and young people about LGBTQ+ rights, then, should they ever face discrimination, they will know that you will stand up and support them if they ever need you to.

5 Respect their agency

It can be tremendously difficult to watch a young person make a choice that could hurt them. Unfortunately, for so many young LGBTQ+ people, the choice to come out is such choice. For that reason, if you are the carer of that young person, it can be tempting to advise them on a path that you perceive will lead to less danger. Of course, it's completely natural to worry, especially given everything we've learnt together in this chapter, but if your response to a young person coming out is to caution them to fly under the radar, then that can come across as asking them to suppress their identity. That can cause internalized homophobia, which can have a dramatic impact on their mental health.

When a young person comes out, it's important to remember how much has gone into their decision to do that and how, often, it takes tremendous strength and courage. They deserve to be celebrated, supported and respected in their choice. The world may not always be respectful, so be sure that you always are.

Summary

In this chapter, we have looked at how the discrimination and challenges facing young LGBTQ+ people today are contributing to their experiencing mental ill health. In helping young LGBTQ+ people to recognize us as allies, we need to make sure that we are engaging with parts of culture that represent and support the LGBTQ+ community.

Self-reflection question

Take a moment to think about TV programmes or films you like that feature LGBTQ+ people's stories. (What I mean here are those that show a fully rounded person rather than a casual stereotype.) Alternatively, maybe you could think about books you like that have been written by LGBTQ+ people or music.

Self-reflection activity

Make a list of your answers to the self-reflection question. Is your list longer than you expected or shorter? Is there anything on your list that you'd like to share with your child or young person and discuss?

If your list is shorter, why do you think that is? Are there TV programmes and films that you have considered watching but haven't because they are LGBTQ+ stories? How do you feel about watching, reading and listening to more work created by LGBTQ+ people?

Summary
Keeping up in a changing world

You are more than where you've been.
You are not your history
So now it's time to break the mould.
Step into your destiny.
Lily-Jo, song 'Unstoppable'

In the process of doing my research for this book, I stumbled on the following quote. Young people, Aristotle (*Rhetoric*, 2.12, 1389a16 – 34) says:

> are trusting, because they have not yet often been cheated. They are hopeful; nature warms their blood as though with excess of wine; and besides that they have as yet met with few disappointments . . . They are high-minded, because they have not yet been humbled by life and they are inexperienced in the force of necessity; moreover, there is high-mindedness in thinking oneself worthy of great things, a feeling which belongs to one who is hopeful. They would always rather do noble deeds than useful ones.

'How interesting,' I thought, 'that people are so concerned about upcoming generations!' The quote was redolent to me of articles I had read about Gen Z. Then I realized that the quote was from the great Greek philosopher. He wrote those words more than *2,000 years ago*. The humour and irony were not lost on me. All these thousands of years later, we are still wrestling with a generation gap. We are still struggling to understand our children and young people. That has been the motivation behind this book – the need to understand and help other adults understand just what kinds of trials children and young people are facing and what kind of world they are living in. At times, it has felt like an uphill struggle.

I clearly remember being an adolescent myself, arguing with my dad about what it was appropriate to wear to go out with my friends to the local youth club. I remember shaking my head at my dad's lack of 'cool' and thinking to myself that I would never be so disconnected if I had children. Now, I am a mum to a Gen Z boy who is a TikTok prodigy and a Gen Alpha daughter who has never lived in a time without apps, phones that play videos and the Internet.

Even though I spend time with more young people than most adults my own age and I am privileged to make meaningful connections with them as part of my work, I am always aware that the world they are living in now is so different from the one I knew when I was growing up. My children have no experience of landline phones. I used to read magazines to follow celebrities and fashion, and wait eagerly for the next episode of *Coronation Street* to be on the TV. For my children, all those experiences are available to them at the touch of a screen, carried in their pocket, always on. My daughter, a child of Gen Alpha, has only ever lived in a world where glass is intrinsically linked to interaction. It is why, sometimes, toddlers of Gen Alpha will try to make the 'swipe' motion on windowpanes. My son's world is full of devices that were still the stuff of science fiction when he was born – driverless cars, watches that record your heart rate, even home robots in the form of Alexa and Siri.

There can be such fear involved in being a parent in today's ultra-modern world. How can we prepare our children and young people for the world of their future, which will certainly look radically different from the one we live in now? How can we protect their mental health and give them tools to develop their resilience when we have no idea what they are or will be facing?

Even now we have reached the end of this book, I cannot provide reassurance that I have given you all the tools you might need to cope with every possible circumstance. As quickly as things become relevant, they become irrelevant again. Perhaps in five years, I will kick myself for not anticipating the wider mental health impact of something that today seems relatively insignificant. The world is always changing, new traumatic experiences will emerge, new Internet trends and fads will have unforeseen impacts on our mental well-being. The future, as it always has been, is impossible to predict.

That said, there is some comfort for us all in that fact for, just as the world is always changing and moving at a pace so rapid that we can barely keep up, our mental health research and understanding is also developing. For example, in the First World War, soldiers came back from the front exhibiting symptoms of what was called 'shell shock'. They were young men who brought the war home with them, experiencing it over and over again inside their heads. By the time the Second World War came around, it was no longer called shell shock but had been renamed 'combat fatigue' or 'war neurosis'. In 1972, further research led to psychiatrist Chaim Shatan coining the term 'post-Vietnam syndrome', used to describe the long-term mental health impacts of war. Finally, in 1980, 'post-traumatic stress disorder' became a formal diagnosis. Today, 'post-traumatic stress disorder' is a formally accepted condition that can result from the effects not only of war, sexual assault or traumatic world events but also is beginning to be diagnosed as a result of what is called 'invisible wounding', caused by racism and other such traumatic events. It's a constantly evolving condition as the psychiatric community learns and understands more about the impact of trauma on the human brain and how the brain responds in everyday life too.

This example of the development of understanding and knowledge gives me tremendous hope. It tells me that just as I cannot see my children's future in terms of the struggles they may face, I also can't foresee the great medical insights we might gain or uncover that will help them. Mental health research and care are not static. They are always changing. We are always learning how to help others to heal and how to improve how we heal ourselves.

In a way, I hope that, in five years' time, I find myself writing another book like this, taking into account new studies, new surveys, new research and new techniques that will enable us to better help and support our children and young people.

Equally, there is also comfort in knowing that some things have been the same since the dawn of time: Children have always needed soothing and everything I have offered you in this book is based on that simple truth. The reasons for them needing to be soothed may change – in this book we've looked at reasons unique to Gen Z and Gen Alpha, everything from social media causing social anxiety to climate change causing depression – but the fact that they need to be soothed is a constant. We are still mammals with mammalian instincts and, as I bring my children up in a world that seems increasingly disconnected from the truths of the natural world, I find that to be a comforting thought. My children are experiencing a radically different childhood from the one I knew, but they still need to be soothed and to be taught how to soothe, so that, as healthy, mentally resilient adults, they will be able to self-soothe and regulate their emotions appropriately. All we are doing, ultimately, is helping them to grow into healthy, emotionally independent adults – something that parents and carers have been doing for hundreds of years. Even when the world is changing radically, that remains true.

Writing this book has been a tremendous process for me. Not only have I learnt a lot from my research and our surveys that will have a positive impact on the Lily-Jo Project and the way we teach and deliver mental health projects in schools worldwide but it has also changed the way I parent. There is a big difference, it turns out, between what I know as a counsellor and mental health professional and how I conduct my daily life. It has been a privilege to spend so much time thinking about how I parent and examining my methods and the reasons behind them. Aside from all the techniques and tips that I have provided in this book, I have a few more final thoughts – not as a professional but purely as a person with children I am trying to soothe, love and grow into strong adults.

Caring for Gen Z and Gen Alpha children and young people – top five tips

1 Believe and value their perspective

One of the best things I did when writing this book was that I spent some time listening to my children's perspectives. For the book to work, I needed their unvarnished opinions. I needed to test that the research we had done held up, but I also needed to see if they agreed with the outcomes of studies or the suggestions given in the books that I had read. To do that, I needed to listen without an agenda, so I could simply *know* what they thought, felt or did.

It was a bit of a revelation. I realized that, so often when we listen to our children and young people, we do not necessarily value their opinions or believe them. So often we easily jump to conclusions, saying things like, 'They're only angry because they're tired' or 'They only think that because they're stressed.' It's totally normal, of course, because we are experts on the children and young people we care for and we don't only want to understand, we also want to make it better. If a child is angry because they are tired, we can make sure that they have an early night and solve the problem. Yet, when we do that, we are inadvertently showing them that we do not believe or value their interpretation of their own feelings. We might be right (they may really be tired), but it does not make them less angry. It does not make the anger feel less real. We are accidentally dismissing their own assertions about their reality.

It's such a little thing, but when we change our language and say, 'I understand that you are angry, do you think you could tell me a little more about why you are feeling that way?', we give our children and young people the message that they can express their real emotions and perspective to us without fear of dismissal. We show them that we will listen and we will hear them and their perspective will be valued. We demonstrate that we will love them precisely as they are. A child or young person who knows that they are loved and valued is more likely to feel comfortable with being open about their negative emotions and speak up when they are struggling with their mental ill health.

2 Value and model emotional vulnerability

Something else that has struck me in the course of writing of this book, as mentioned earlier, is how much children and young people watch us on a daily basis. Our culture is one that places a premium on watching – or 'following' – and I have realized how those observation skills are innate in our children and young people. They've been brought up with advertisers pushing them into mimicking people they see online or on TV, mimicking their hair, their clothes, their attitude and even their spending habits. They are watching us too. They listen to how we speak about others, how we speak about ourselves and our own bodies, how we talk about our own mental health.

When I was growing up, mental health was not something that was talked about, and my parents did not model emotional vulnerability towards us children. No doubt they wanted to appear like strong caregivers, immovable parental figures who I could rely on at all times. I don't blame them at all because I understand the reasoning behind it completely.

I never want my children to feel like I am unstable or burdened by my emotions in a way that hurts them. Yet, I have also come to recognize the importance of modelling emotional vulnerability to them. I do not break down in front of them, but I am open with them about days when I am feeling down. I try to be honest, saying things like, 'Today, I am feeling a little depressed but that's OK. It's OK to have days when you don't feel good.' I let myself be a little vulnerable, take a little risk, but I know that I am giving them a language in which they can speak about mental health. I am normalizing it for them and demonstrating the value of emotional vulnerability, so they can feel safe to be vulnerable with me too.

3 Recognize their autonomy

One of the most challenging parts of writing this book has been being open about the ways in which my family has struggled. After all, I am a mental health professional – if anyone should be able to have a mentally healthy family it should be me, right? Yet, I have learnt that, ultimately, this isn't about me. Their struggles are not about me. My children might benefit from my professional insights, but they are not mini versions of me. They are growing up in a totally different environment, at a completely different point in history. They are their own autonomous beings and they are making their own decisions that will have various impacts on their own mental health and I have to allow those things to happen.

It can be hard, when caring for a child or young person, to accept that they will not always behave in the way you would in a given situation. You might do everything you can, perhaps even read a whole book dedicated to the subject of mental health, and they still might shut you out and ignore you.

Autonomy is a huge part of mental development and building resilience in children and young people. When we try to take that autonomy away from then, when we try to force them into communicating or behaving in certain ways, we are, in fact, hindering that from happening. We are also eroding their trust in us. When a child or young person is struggling with a mental health issue, forcing them to 'deal' with it in the way we see fit only pushes them further away from our help.

4 Accept your limitations

Sometimes, you can't help but feel like a total failure. It could be that your child needs a tutor or additional support in the classroom, or it could be that the child or young person in your care is self-harming or confesses that they are depressed. At such moments, you might feel completely out of your depth as you realize that, sometimes, you can't provide your child or young person with everything they need. It feels like the worst failure imaginable; it feels like every decision you have made has led to this moment when you somehow, horribly, let your child down.

It is so important when these things occur to recognize what is truly happening at that moment – that it is not about us and our limitations; it is not about our capability or inability. We are simply not enough right now; we cannot give them exactly what they need to thrive.

We can take that badly, resist the truth and continue to struggle to provide our children or young people with what they need, or we can accept our limitations and accept that, sometimes, our children need resources beyond what we can provide. We can seek help from others. It does not make us bad parents or carers to recognize that; it makes us human. We are also better carers and parents when we are realistic about our limitations.

5 Be kind to your own mind

Writing about the mental resilience and wellness of children and young people has made me more aware of my own mental resilience and how important it is to take care of my own mind, as well as my children's. Much like how, in an aircraft, they suggest you place the oxygen mask on yourself before your child, it is so important that, as adults who care for children and young people, we are not only modelling good mental health practices in our lives but we are also taking care of ourselves.

The pandemic brought this truth home to me with a roaring conviction. I struggled mentally, but I needed to allow myself to struggle and give myself time to heal. It was essential not only for my own mental well-being but also the mental well-being of my family and those I provide care for. I am a better mother when I am aware of my own mental health. I am a kinder person when I am kind to my own mind. I am a better listener when I am listening to my own needs. I am a better provider to those around me when I make sure that my mental health is provided for.

So, please, be aware of your own mental space. Ask yourself what revitalizes you mentally, what gives you peace and tranquillity, then build small moments into your day to give yourself that time. Use this book as an opportunity not only for learning but also to reflect on your own mental well-being and journey and use the tools to build your own resilience.

***

We cannot stop the world from changing. We cannot shelter children from the ills of the world. We cannot anticipate and protect them from every threat imaginable – we would drive ourselves into the ground if we even tried. We can now, however, face the future with hope, armed with the tools and information we need to help our young people become the best they can be. I for one, can't wait to see the future they create.

***

Please visit <www.thelilyjoproject.com/book> for bonus content, updates and to share your thoughts and experiences.

Acknowledgements

People often say to me, 'I don't know how you do it all!' and the truth is, 'I don't!' I am blessed to be surrounded by an incredible family and brilliant friends, who believe in me and have supported my journey from the beginning.

I want to start by thanking my parents, who provided a safe and nurturing environment for me to grow in, and who to this day continue to support me and my family. I love you both very much.

My handsome, brilliant husband, Dave. My soulmate. Your passion for this book has been the fuel I've needed when imposter syndrome has crept in. Thank you for making me a parent and gifting me the most incredible children. Journeying through this life with you is a total honour.

Thank you to my beautiful children, Dylan and Nico, for teaching me so many lessons included in this book, and the many that are not featured here. I love you both so much, and I am so proud of you both.

Christine, mother-in-law of all mothers-in-law! Thank you for being a beautiful example of motherhood. You make me laugh so much, and your gratitude for life, regardless of huge adversity, is inspiring. Jim would be very proud of the woman you continue to become.

To all my brothers and sisters, Adam, Hannah, Rob, Becky, Andy, Olivia, Betsy, Helen, Debs, Rach, Matt and the ever-growing tribe of beautiful nieces and nephews: I'm so grateful for you all.

To my longstanding team at the Lily-Jo Project, Emma Hinds, Shelby Hale, Peter Bonnebaigt, my freelancers and the generous donors: thank you for catching my vision and turning it into a reality. Without your generosity, energy and consistency, we wouldn't be able to help the thousands of children, teens and adults whom we do each year.

Thank you to Elizabeth Neep, Jo Pountney and the team at SPCK. It's been a pleasure to work with you guys and bring this work into the world with your support and expertise. I'm hugely grateful for the opportunity.

To every person on my mailing list, every follower on social media: thank you. Together we can achieve the goal to promote and provide credible mental health resources for all.

Last but not least, to the reader: thank you for reading this book. I hope that it has left you feeling empowered to be the best caregiver to those in your world. I believe in you.

Any thoughts, feelings and comments can be emailed to me directly here: lilyjo@thelilyjoproject.com

Notes

Introduction

1 NHS England, 'Mental health', NHS England (n.d.), <www.england.nhs.uk/mental-health/#:~:text=One%20in %20four%20adults%20and,care%20for%20people%20who %20do.> (accessed September 2022).

2 Mental Health Foundation, 'Stigma and discrimination', Mental Health Foundation (n.d.), <www.mentalhealth .org.uk/a-to-z/s/stigma-and-discrimination> (accessed September 2022).

3 World Health Organization (WHO), 'Suicide: One person dies every 40 seconds', WHO (9 September 2019), <www .who.int/news/item/09-09-2019-suicide-one-person-dies -every-40-seconds> (accessed September 2022).

4 Samaritans, 'Latest suicide data', Samaritans (2021), <www.samaritans.org/about-samaritans/research-policy /suicide-facts-and-figures/latest-suicide-data> (accessed September 2022).

5 Mental Health Foundation, 'Children and young people', Mental Health Foundation (n.d.), <www.mentalhealth.org .uk/explore-mental-health/a-z-topics/children-and-young -people> (accessed September 2022).

6 Young Minds, 'Mental health statistics', Young Minds (n.d.), <www.youngminds.org.uk/about-us/media-centre /mental-health-statistics> (accessed September 2022). See also NHS Digital, 'Mental health of children and young people in England, 2017', NHS Digital (22 November

2018), <https://digital.nhs.uk/data-and-information
/publications/statistical/mental-health-of-children-and
-young-people-in-england/2017/2017>, and update, NHS
Digital, 'Mental health of children and young people in
England, 2021 – wave 2 follow up to the 2017 survey',
NHS Digital (30 September 2021), <https://digital.nhs
.uk/data-and-information/publications/statistical/mental
-health-of-children-and-young-people-in-england/2021
-follow-up-to-the-2017-survey> (accessed September
2022).

1 Generation AO

1 Mental Health Foundation, 'Loneliness during
coronavirus', Mental Health Foundation (17 May 2020),
<www.kesw.org/wp-content/uploads/2020/05/Loneliness
-during-coronavirus-_-Mental-Health-Foundation-pdf
.pdf> (accessed September 2022).

2 M. Dinic, 'Lockdown blues: The impact of coronavirus on
loneliness in Britain', YouGov (4 February 2021), <https://
yougov.co.uk/topics/society/articles-reports/2021/02/04
/lockdown-blues-impact-coronavirus-loneliness-brita>
(accessed September 2022).

3 C. Ibbetson, 'Who are the most lonely people in the
UK?', YouGov (3 October 2019), <yougov.co.uk/topics
/relationships/articles-reports/2019/10/03/young-britons
-are-most-lonely> (accessed September 2022).

4 CommonSense Media, 'New report finds teens
feel addicted to their phones, causing tension at
home', CommonSense Media (3 May 2016), <www
.commonsensemedia.org/press-releases/new-report-finds

-teens-feel-addicted-to-their-phones-causing-tension-at
-home> (accessed September 2022).

5 E. Peper and R. Harvey, 'Digital addiction: Increased
loneliness, anxiety and depression', *NeuroRegulation*, vol. 5,
no. 1 (2018), pp. 3–8, <https://www.neuroregulation.org
/article/view/18189/11842> (accessed September 2022).

6 Peper and Harvey, 'Digital addiction', pp. 3–8.

7 A. Galván, 'The teenage brain: Sensitivity to rewards',
Current Directions in Psychological Science, vol. 22, no. 2
(2013), pp. 90–2, <https://journals.sagepub.com/doi/pdf/10
.1177/0963721413480859> (accessed September 2022).

8 Peper and Harvey, 'Digital addiction', pp. 3–8.

9 M. Pittman, 'Phoneliness: Exploring the relationships
between mobile social media, personality and loneliness',
doctoral dissertation, University of Oregon (June 2017),
<https://core.ac.uk/download/pdf/92864729.pdf> (accessed
September 2022).

10 Our study surveyed 121 students between the ages of
11 and 18 from our local community of Stockport, UK.
Survey and interviews by the Lily-Jo Project (2020), <www
.thelilyjoproject.com/research> (accessed September 2022).

2 Anxiety gone viral

1 Attest, 'UK health and wellbeing report 2020', Attest
(2020), <https://prod-corporate-fe-assets.s3.amazonaws
.com/uploads/2020/04/Attest_UK-Health-Wellbeing
-Report-2020.pdf> (accessed September 2022).

2 N. Racine, B. A. McArthur, J. E. Cooke et al., 'Global
prevalence of depressive and anxiety symptoms
in children and adolescents during COVID-19:

A meta-analysis', *JAMA Pediatrics*, vol. 175, no. 11 (2021), pp. 1142–50, <https://jamanetwork.com/journals /jamapediatrics/fullarticle/2782796> (accessed September 2022).

3 Survey and interviews by the Lily-Jo Project (2020), <www.thelilyjoproject.com/research> (accessed September 2022).

4 R. Ziatdinov and J. Cilliers, 'Generation Alpha: Understanding the next cohort of university students', *European Journal of Contemporary Education*, vol. 10, no. 3 (2021), pp. 783–9), <www.ziatdinov-lab.com/manuscripts /generation-alpha-ziatdinov-cilliers> (accessed September 2022).

5 K. Bialik and R. Fry, 'Millennial life: How young adulthood today compares with prior generations', Pew Research Center (14 February 2019), <www.pewresearch .org/social-trends/2019/02/14/millennial-life-how-young -adulthood-today-compares-with-prior-generations-2> (accessed September 2022).

6 Survey and interviews by the Lily-Jo Project (2020).

7 N. Patel, 'Who is Generation Alpha, and why are they important to marketers', Neil Patel (n.d.), <https://neilpatel .com/blog/generation-alpha/#:~:text=Gen%20Alpha %20already%20uses%20social,success%20with%20this %20burgeoning%20generation> (accessed September 2022).

8 L1ght, 'Rising levels of hate speech and online toxicity during this time of crisis', L1ght (April 2020), <https:// l1ght.com/Toxicity_during_coronavirus_Report-L1ght .pdf?fbclid=IwAR12yPh-GIi1Ur1qwwZoCuu4nP2zG5dLxs

590Exli5UXYORQCWp3w_ko1MQ> (accessed September 2022).

9 M. McCrindle, 'Generation next: Meet Gen Z and the Alphas', McCrindle Research (n.d.), <https://mccrindle .com.au/uncategorized/generation-next-meet-gen-z-and -the-alphas> (accessed September 2022).

3 Pandemic pressure

1 M. McCrindle and A. Fell, 'Understanding the impact of COVID-19 on the emerging generations', McCrindle Research (May 2020), <https:// mccrindle.com.au/wp-content/uploads/reports/COVID19- Emerging-Generations-Report-2020.pdf> (accessed September 2022).

2 Young Minds, 'Coronavirus: Impact on young people with mental health needs', Young Minds (March 2020), <www.youngminds.org.uk/media/xq2dnc0d/youngminds -coronavirus-report-march2020.pdf>, and see also the report on its follow-up survey, 'Coronavirus: Impact on young people with mental health needs: Survey 2: Summer 2020', Young Minds (July 2020), <www.youngminds.org .uk/media/355gyqcd/coronavirus-report-summer-2020 -final.pdf> (accessed September 2022).

3 Survey and interviews by the Lily-Project (2020), <www .thelilyjoproject.com/research> (accessed September 2022).

4 Office for National Statistics (ONS), 'Coronavirus and the social impacts on Great Britain: 14 May 2020', ONS (14 May 2020), <www.ons.gov.uk /peoplepopulationandcommunity/healthandsocialcare /healthandwellbeing/bulletins/coronavirusandthesoci

alimpactsongreatbritain/14may2020#homeschooling>
(accessed September 2022).

5 Survey and interviews by the Lily-Jo Project (2020).

6 P. Tucker and C. S. Czapla, 'Post-COVID stress disorder: Another emerging consequence of the global pandemic', *Psychiatric Times*, vol. 38, no. 1 (8 January 2021), <www .psychiatrictimes.com/view/post-covid-stress-disorder -emerging-consequence-global-pandemic> (accessed September 2022).

7 L. Liang, T. Gao, H. Ren et al., 'Post-traumatic stress disorder and psychological distress in Chinese youths following the COVID-19 emergency', *Journal of Health Psychology*, vol. 25, no. 9 (6 July 2020), <https://journals .sagepub.com/doi/full/10.1177/1359105320937057> (accessed September 2022).

4 Bodies made digital

1 R. Adams, 'Social media urged to take "moment to reflect" after girl's death', *The Guardian* (30 January 2019), <www .theguardian.com/media/2019/jan/30/social-media-urged -to-take-moment-to-reflect-after-girls-death> (accessed September 2022).

2 Survey and interviews by the Lily-Jo Project (2020), <www.thelilyjoproject.com/research> (accessed September 2022).

3 University College London (UCL), 'Initial findings from the Millennium Cohort Study Age 14 Sweep', UCL (2017), <https://cls.ucl.ac.uk/cls-studies/millennium-cohort-study /mcs-age-14-sweep> (accessed September 2022).

4 P. Stallard, M. Spears, A. A. Montgomery, et al.,

'Self-harm in young adolescents (12–16 years): Onset and short-term continuation in a community sample', *BMC Psychiatry*, vol. 13, article no. 328 (2013), <https:// bmcpsychiatry.biomedcentral.com/articles/10.1186/1471-244X-13-328> (accessed September 2022).

5 V. Otkan, 'Self-harm behaviour in adolescents: Body image and self-esteem', *Journal of Psychologists and Counsellors in Schools*, vol. 27, no. 2 (8 June 2017), <www.cambridge.org/core/journals/journal-of-psychologists-and-counsellors-in-schools/article/selfharm-behaviour-in-adolescents-body-image-and-selfesteem/2EFA88A3516BB08FEAB783C76FFBD89E> (accessed September 2022).

6 Young Minds and the Children's Society, 'Safety net: Cyberbullying's impact on young people's mental health: Inquiry report', Young Minds (2018), <www.youngminds.org.uk/media/dp0mu4l5/pcr144b_social_media_cyberbullying_inquiry_full_report.pdf > (accessed September 2022).

7 F. Marcheselli, 'England's first estimates of body dysmorphic disorder prevalence in children and young people', NatCen (17 December 2018), <www.natcen.ac.uk/blog/englands-first-estimates-of-body-dysmorphic-disorder-prevalence-in-children-and-young-people> (accessed September 2022).

8 K. Phillips, 'Prevalence of BDD', International OCD Foundation (n.d.), <https://bdd.iocdf.org/professionals/prevalence/#:~:text=Body%20Dysmorphic%20Disorder%20affects%201.7,United%20States%20alone%20have%20BDD> (accessed September 2022).

9 N. C. Dewall, G. Macdonald, G. D. Webster, et al., 'Acetaminophen reduces social pain: Behavioural and neural evidence', *Psychological Science*, vol. 21, no. 7 (July 2010), <https://pubmed.ncbi.nlm.nih.gov/20548058> (accessed September 2022).

10 C. Arnold, 'Why self-harm?', Aeon (13 October 2014), <https://aeon.co/essays/how-self-harm-provokes-the-brain-into-feeling-better> (accessed September 2022).

11 Young Minds and the Children's Society, 'Safety Net'.

12 T. Locke, '86% of young people say they want to post social media content for money', makeit CNBC (8 November 2019), <www.cnbc.com/2019/11/08/study-young-people-want-to-be-paid-influencers.html> (accessed September 2022).

13 A. Pitman, 'Understanding and preventing copycat suicides', BMC Series blog (5 March 2018), <https://blogs.biomedcentral.com/bmcseriesblog/2018/03/05/understanding-and-preventing-copycat-suicides> (accessed September 2022).

14 Mental Health Foundation, 'The truth about self-harm: For young people and their friends and families', Mental Health Foundation (29 February 2016), <www.mentalhealth.org.uk/sites/default/files/2022-07/MHF-The-truth-about-self-harm-guide.pdf> (accessed September 2022).

5 Depression in a dying world

1 Office for National Statistics (ONS), 'Young people's well-being in the UK: 2020', ONS (2 October 2020), <www.ons.gov.uk/peoplepopulationandcommunity/wellbeing

/bulletins/youngpeopleswellbeingintheuk/2020#:~:text=
There%20is%20evidence%20of%20increasing,five%20
years%20earlier%20(26%25)> (accessed September 2022).

2 H. Bould, B. Mars, P. Moran, et al., 'Rising suicide
rates among adolescents in England and Wales, *The
Lancet*, vol. 394, no. 10193 (18 June 2019), pp. 116–17,
<www.thelancet.com/journals/lancet/article/PIIS0140-
6736(19)31102-X/fulltext> (accessed September 2022).

3 S. Clayton, C. M. Manning, K. Krygsman, et al.,
'Mental health and our changing climate: Impacts,
implications, and guidance', American Psychological
Association (APA) and ecoAmerica (March 2017), <www
.apa.org/news/press/releases/2017/03/mental-health
-climate.pdf> (accessed September 2022).

4 Blue Shield of California, 'Gen Z youth say climate change
is adversely affecting their physical and mental health in
new national survey by Blue Shield of California', Blue
Shield of California (15 April 2021), <https://news.
blueshieldca.com/2021/04/15/NextGenGoals> (accessed
September 2022).

5 United Nations (UN), 'Only 11 years left to prevent
irreversible damage from climate change, speakers
warn during General Assembly high-level meeting', UN
(28 March 2019), <www.un.org/press/en/2019/ga12131.
doc.htm> (accessed September 2022).

6 S. J. Ray, 'Generation Z is "traumatised" by climate
change – and they're the key to fighting it', *Fortune*
(19 August 2020), <https://fortune.com/2020/08/19
/generation-z-climate-change-activism> (accessed
September 2022).

7 Survey and interviews by the Lily-Jo Project (2020), <www
.thelilyjoproject.com/research> (accessed September 2022).

8 F. Ward, *Like There's No Tomorrow: Climate crisis,
eco-anxiety and God* (Durham: Sacristy Press, 2020), p. 8.

9 R. Zlatanova, 'The newest climate report looks grim:
Here's why we still have hope', World Wildlife Fund
(WWF) (4 April 2022), <www.worldwildlife.org/stories
/the-newest-climate-report-looks-grim-here-s-why-we-still
-have-hope> (accessed September 2022).

10 Martin Luther King Junior, address given in Washington,
DC, February 1968, in C. S. King, *Martin Luther King: In
my own words: Selected and introduced by Coretta Scott
King* (London: Hodder & Stoughton, 2002).

6 Global grief

1 S. Schrobsdorff, 'Teen depression and anxiety: Why the
kids are not alright', *Time*, vol. 188, no. 19 (27 October
2016), <https://time.com/magazine/us/4547305/november
-7th-2016-vol-188-no-19-u-s> (accessed September 2022).

2 Schrobsdorff, 'Teen depression and anxiety'.

3 R. Janfaza, '"We're tired of waiting": Gen Z is ready for a
revolution', CNN Politics (22 June 2020), <https://edition
.cnn.com/2020/06/16/politics/genz-voters-2020-election
/index.html> (accessed September 2022).

4 Survey and interviews by the Lily-Jo Project (2020), <www
.thelilyjoproject.com/research> (accessed September 2022).

5 Quoted in C. Weaver, 'Pandemic helps "Generation Z"
ignite a movement', *Financial Times* (12 June 2020), <www
.ft.com/content/effbfc03-61f3-4f99-910c-8befe46a6c08>
(accessed September 2022).

6 R. Janfaza, '"We're tired of waiting"'.

7 R. Janfaza, '"We're tired of waiting"'.

7 Fear in the fluid generation

1 P. Tassi, 'Netflix's "Heartstopper" is its highest-scoring critic and audience hit in ages', *Forbes* (28 April 2022), <www.forbes.com/sites/paultassi/2022/04/28/netflixs-heartstopper-is-its-highest-scoring-critic-and-audience-hit-in-ages/?sh=7b0ab85233b6> (accessed September 2022).

2 H. Clayton, 'Why is the LGBTQ+ community disproportionately affected by mental health problems and suicide?', University of Manchester (6 October 2020), <https://sites.manchester.ac.uk/carms/2020/10/06/why-is-the-lgbtq-community-disproportionately-affected-by-mental-health-problems-and-suicide/#_edn14> (accessed September 2022).

3 Trevor Project, '2022 national survey on LGBTQ youth mental health', Trevor Project (May 2022), <www.thetrevorproject.org/survey-2022> (accessed September 2022).

4 D. Reynolds, 'Study: Half of Gen Z believes the gender binary is outdated', Advocate (24 February 2021), <www.advocate.com/business/2021/2/24/study-half-gen-z-believes-gender-binary-outdated> (accessed September 2022).

5 K. Wickman, 'Why has everyone fallen in love with Netflix's *Heartstopper*?', *Vanity Fair* (6 May 2022), <www.vanityfair.com/hollywood/2022/05/heartstopper-netflix-alice-oseman-interview#:~:text=The%20show%2C

%20which%20premiered%20in,April%2022%20and %20the%2025th> (accessed September 2022).

6 P. MacInnes, 'Jake Daniels becomes first UK male footballer to come out as gay since 1990', *The Guardian* (16 May 2022), <www.theguardian.com/football/2022/may /16/jake-daniels-becomes-first-uk-male-footballer-to-come -out-as-gay-since-1990> (accessed September 2022).

7 'Victims' lives remembered: Students, partners, trusted friends', *New York Times* (14 June 2016), <www.nytimes .com/interactive/projects/cp/us/orlando-shooting-victims /akyra-monet-murray> (accessed September 2022).

8 H. S. Stevens, 'Significant rise in anti-LGBTQ+ hate crime since 2015', EachOther (25 October 2021), <https:// eachother.org.uk/significant-rise-in-anti-lgbtq-hate-crime -since-2015/> (accessed September 2022).

9 Stevens, 'Significant rise in anti-LGBTQ+ hate crime since 2015'.

10 Stonewall, 'LGBT in Britain: Hate crime and discrimination', Stonewall (September 2017), <www .stonewall.org.uk/lgbt-britain-hate-crime-and -discrimination> (accessed September 2022).

11 Notre Dame Catholic Sixth Form College Student Newspaper, 'Opinion: Do the police care about queer people?', Notre Dame Catholic Sixth Form College (21 March 2022), <www.notredamecoll.ac.uk/news/opinion -do-police-care-about-queer-people> (accessed September 2022).

12 B. Ghafoori, Y. Caspi, C. Salgado et al., 'Global perspectives on the trauma of hate-based violence', An International Society for Traumatic Stress Studies briefing

paper, International Society for Traumatic Stress Studies (2019), <https://istss.org/ISTSS_Main/media/Documents /ISTSS-Global-Perspectives-on-the-Trauma-of-Hate-Based -Violence-Briefing-Paper_1.pdf> (accessed September 2022).

13 Ghafoori et al., *Global perspectives on the trauma of hate-based violence*.

14 Stonewall, 'The experiences of LGBTQ+ children and young people', Stonewall (n.d.), <www.stonewall.org.uk /experiences-lgbtq-children-and-young-people> (accessed September 2022).

15 Stonewall, 'Stonewall report reveals impact of discrimination on health of LGBT people', Stonewall (n.d.), <www.stonewall.org.uk/about-us/media-releases /stonewall-report-reveals-impact-discrimination-health -lgbt-people> (accessed September 2022).

16 C. Somerville, 'Unhealthy attitudes: The treatment of LGBT people within the health and social care services', Stonewall (11 September 2015), <www.stonewall.org .uk/system/files/unhealthy_attitudes.pdf> (accessed September 2022).

17 Stonewall, 'The experiences of LGBTQ+ children and young people'.

18 Trevor Project, 'National survey on LGBTQ youth mental health 2021', Trevor Project (2021), <www.thetrevorproject .org/survey-2021> (accessed September 2022).

Select bibliography and further reading

Books

Brotheridge, C., *The Anxiety Solution: A quieter mind, a calmer you* (London: Penguin, 2017).

Brotheridge, C., *The Confidence Solution: The essential guide to boosting self-esteem, reducing anxiety and feeling confident* (London: Penguin, 2021).

Caught, A., *Queer Up: An uplifting guide to LGBTQ+ love, life and mental health* (London: Walker Books, 2022).

Elmore, T., *Generation Z Unfiltered: Facing nine hidden challenges of the most anxious population* (Atlanta, GA: Poet Gardner, 2019).

Elmore, T., *The Pandemic Population: Eight strategies to help Generation Z rediscover hope after coronavirus* (Atlanta, GA: Poet Gardner, 2020).

Freeman, J., *Cover Up: Understanding self-harm* (Dublin: Veritas, 2011).

Kolk, B. van der, *The Body Keeps the Score: Mind, brain and body in the transformation of trauma* (London: Penguin, 2014).

McCrindle, M. and Fell, A. with Buckerfield, S., *Generation Alpha: Understanding our children and helping them thrive* (London: Headline Home, 2021).

McCrindle, M., with Wolfinger, E., *The ABC of XYZ: Understanding the global generations* (3rd edition, Bella Vista, New South Wales: McCrindle Research, 2014).

Malcolm, Hannah (ed.), *Words for a Dying World: Stories of grief and courage from the global Church* (London: SCM Press, 2020).

Ray, S. J., *A Field Guide to Climate Anxiety: How to keep your cool on a warming planet* (Oakland: University of California Press, 2020).

Reading, S., *The Self-care Revolution: Smart habits and simple practices to allow you to flourish* (London: Aster, 2017).

Ward, F., *Like There's No Tomorrow: Climate crisis, eco-anxiety and God* (Durham: Sacristy Press, 2020).

Academic and scientific journals

BMC Psychiatry
Current Direction in Psychological Science
European Journal of Contemporary Education
JAMA Paediatrics
Journal of Health Psychology
Journal of Psychologists and Counsellors in Schools
NeuroRegulation Journal
Lancet, The
Psychiatric Times
Psychological Science

Surveys and reports

Attest, 'UK health and wellbeing report 2020', Attest (2020), <https://prod-corporate-fe-assets.s3.amazonaws.com /uploads/2020/04/Attest_UK-Health-Wellbeing-Report -2020.pdf> (accessed September 2022).

Bialik, K. and Fry, R. 'Millennial life: How young adulthood today compares with prior generations', Pew Research

Center (14 February 2019), <www.pewresearch.org/social
-trends/2019/02/14/millennial-life-how-young-adulthood
-today-compares-with-prior-generations-2> (accessed
September 2022).

Blue Shield of California, 'Blue Shield of California NextGen
climate survey', Blue Shield of California (2021), <https://
s3.amazonaws.com/cms.ipressroom.com/347/files/20213
/BlueShieldCA_NextGenSurveyReport_FINAL.pdf>
(accessed September 2022).

Clayton, S., Manning, C. M., Krygsman, K. and Speiser,
M., 'Mental health and our changing climate: Impacts,
implications, and Guidance', American Psychological
Association (APA) and ecoAmerica (March 2017), <www
.apa.org/news/press/releases/2017/03/mental-health-climate
.pdf> (accessed September 2022).

Ghafoori, B., Caspi, Y., Salgado, C., et al., 'Global perspectives
on the trauma of hate-based violence: An International
Society for Traumatic Stress Studies briefing paper',
International Society for Traumatic Stress Studies (2019),
<https://istss.org/ISTSS_Main/media/Documents/ISTSS
-Global-Perspectives-on-the-Trauma-of-Hate-Based
-Violence-Briefing-Paper_1.pdf> (accessed September 2022).

Hunte, B., 'Exclusive: Massive rise in anti-LGBTQ hate crime
reports in UK', VICE World News (15 August 2022),
<www.vice.com/en/article/93akz3/lgbtq-hate-crimes>
(accessed September 2022).

Ibbetson, C., 'Who are the most lonely people in the UK?',
YouGov (3 October 2019), <https://yougov.co.uk/topics
/society/articles-reports/2019/10/03/young-britons-are
-most-lonely> (accessed September 2022).

L1ght, 'Rising levels of hate speech and online toxicity during this time of crisis', L1ght (April 2020), <https://l1ght.com/Toxicity_during_coronavirus_Report-L1ght.pdf?fbclid=IwAR12yPh-GIi1Ur1qwwZoCuu4nP2zG5dLxs590Exli5UXYORQCWp3w_ko1MQ> (accessed September 2022).

McCrindle, M., and Fell, A., 'Understanding the impact of COVID-19 on the emerging generations', McCrindle Research (May 2020), <https://mccrindle.com.au/wp-content/uploads/reports/COVID19-Emerging-Generations-Report-2020.pdf> (accessed September 2022).

Office for National Statistics (ONS), 'Young people's well-being in the UK: 2020', ONS (2 October 2020), <www.ons.gov.uk/peoplepopulationandcommunity/wellbeing/bulletins/youngpeopleswellbeingintheuk/2020#:~:text=There%20is%20evidence%20of%20increasing,five%20years%20earlier%20(26%25)> (accessed September 2022).

Somerville, C., 'Unhealthy attitudes: The treatment of LGBT people within the health and social care services', Stonewall (11 September 2015), <www.stonewall.org.uk/system/files/unhealthy_attitudes.pdf> (accessed September 2022).

Stonewall, 'The experiences of LGBTQ+ children and young people', Stonewall (n.d.), <https://www.stonewall.org.uk/experiences-lgbtq-children-and-young-people> (accessed September 2022).

Stonewall, 'LGBT in Britain: Hate crime and discrimination', Stonewall (2017), <www.stonewall.org.uk/lgbt-britain-hate-crime-and-discrimination> (accessed September 2022).

Trevor Project, 'National survey on LGBTQ youth mental

health 2021', Trevor Project (2021), <www.thetrevorproject
.org/survey-2021> (accessed September 2022).

University College London (UCL), 'Initial findings from the
Millennium Cohort Study Age 14 Sweep', UCL (2017),
<https://cls.ucl.ac.uk/cls-studies/millennium-cohort-study
/mcs-age-14-sweep> (accessed September 2022).

Young Minds, 'Coronavirus: Impact on young people with
mental health needs', Young Minds (March 2020), <www
.youngminds.org.uk/media/xq2dnc0d/youngminds
-coronavirus-report-march2020.pdf>, and see also the
report on its follow-up survey, 'Coronavirus: Impact on
young people with mental health needs: Survey 2: Summer
2020' (July 2020), <www.youngminds.org.uk/media
/355gyqcd/coronavirus-report-summer-2020-final.pdf>
(accessed September 2022).

Young Minds and the Children's Society, 'Safety net:
Cyberbullying's impact on young people's mental health:
Inquiry report', Young Minds and the Children's Society
(2018), <www.youngminds.org.uk/media/dp0mu4l5
/pcr144b_social_media_cyberbullying_inquiry_full
_report.pdf > (accessed September 2022).